ESCAPE FROM LATVIA

Escape from LATVIA

ONE FAMILY'S ESCAPE FROM LATVIA
IN 1944 TO AUSTRALIA IN 1948

VID VIDINS

Dedication

I dedicate this story to my parents, who were displaced from their homeland by war, in fear of their lives, and came to a completely foreign land where they endured alienation and hardship and struggled to survive.

They faced and conquered all the obstacles and challenges that life put before them.

They were also confronted with many surprises. Things that were normal where they came from were "upside down here in Australia".

I also acknowledge, and am thankful to, all those who came before them.

In retrospect, if it wasn't for some of these issues that occurred at the end of World War II – the tough decisions, the sacrifices made – I would never have existed.

I'd like to remind those who come after my wife Wanda and I that no matter what adversity you may face in life, those who came before you also faced major challenges and overcame them as best we could.

This is a true story based on things I was told in parts of conversations and that I overheard in conversations with others, and on my personal lived experiences in Australia and overseas.

I felt a little apprehensive in writing what I have. This was due to my early life experiences. I have learnt that some people tend to quickly label others, only through the perspective they know no matter how narrow that perspective is.

It also provides a possible vision for the future of Australia.

First published in 2026.

National Library of Australia Cataloguing-in-Publication data:

Escape from Latvia: One Family's Escape from Latvia in 1944 to Australia in 1948 / Vid Vidins

Print ISBN 978-1-7646121-0-4

Cover, text design and typesetting: Les Thomas

Book production and editing: Good Prose Studios

A catalogue record for this book is available from the National Library of Australia

Contents

My mother 1

My father 8

Ancient history 11

Latvia and Germany 18

Australia 30

Bowral 39

Work 64

Vidvuds 85

My mother's parents 88

My father's father 96

My brothers 98

Wanda, my wife, and my children 99

Russia, December 1991 104

Riga 113

Revisiting Latvia, 1994 121

Rita, Germany, 2024 129

Reflection on my life and lessons learnt 134

Appendix – Rita's letter 158

My mother

The Russians were rapidly advancing into Latvia towards the end of World War II.

My grandfather Janis (John) on my mother's side had fought the Russian Bolsheviks in the War of Independence in 1919.

He was a landholder and the father of two young daughters, Olga and Helena. He also had two sons, Stanislaus, the youngest, and Constantine, the eldest.

Constantine was injured in the Ukraine fighting with the Germans. He had lain injured in the wheat fields for three days before they found him. He had the option of bleeding to death or using a tourniquet. He chose the latter and put a tourniquet on the leg. His leg then went gangrenous.

The German medics, when they found him, didn't have any more anaesthetic so they gave him a bottle of vodka as a substitute, and sawed off the gangrenous part of his leg in the field while he was drunk but still awake.

On the plane trip to hospital, the medics noticed the gangrene had spread, so they gave him another bottle of vodka and cut off another part of his leg. He survived.

See the Appendix for an email to Constantine from his daughter.

The Russian soldiers had a bad reputation for their treatment of women, especially the young ones they called the "enemy". Women were also regarded as the "spoils of war".

My future mother was 18 years of age and her younger sister was 16.

My grandfather's two daughters, Olga and Helena, left Latvia on foot in the middle of the Northern European winter, when days were only about six hours long, it was snowing and the temperature, according to records, ranged between 2.8 and 9.7 °C during the day and was even colder at night.

They walked to Dresden, over 1100 km away, into Eastern Germany.

There was no fuel and therefore no mechanised transport. They wheeled a small handmade wooden-wheeled handcart made by my grandfather, carrying all their essential possessions and some food. The only water available for drinking and basic washing was made by melting snow.

Olga and Helena got separated from my grandparents in the early confusion and panic of the people trying to leave Dviete, in Latvia. But they had a contingency plan to keep in touch if they got separated.

The wheels of the wooden cart squeaked, so my aunt had put butter on them to minimise the problem. Along the route, there was no available shelter and there were no washing or toilet facilities – Olga and Helana were wearing most of their clothes, especially at night.

Unable to wash themselves or their clothes properly, they became ridden with lice. They were constantly hungry and slept only where they believed it was safe.

They ended up in the refugee centre along with many other refugees to Dresden, in what later became East Germany.

The English and Americans bombed Dresden on 13–15 February 1945. The British bombed at night and Americans bombed during the day. This bombing was later considered a war crime committed by the allies. This was not considered a military objective, and in February 1945 the war was nearly over.

Dresden had more than 100,000 refugees. Some experts say the bombing was to show the Russians that the Allies could reach East Germany and deliver a massive blow to the Russians if they needed to later. Others say it was revenge by the British Arthur "Bomber" Harris for the German bombing of Coventry in England.

Harris was the RAF's Commander-in-Chief. He resisted "precision bombing" of particular facilities and preferred "area bombing" or "carpet bombing". He had ordered the firebombing of Hamburg and the first 1000-night bomber raid of Cologne. Harris never expressed remorse for his actions. He was the sole Commander-in-Chief of the British forces not to become a peer after World War II.

My mother and aunt had to open drums of an unknown substance that generated a dense cloud of smoke when the air raid sirens started and during the bombing. Mum said she had to help her sister with her quota of chemicals. Her younger sister was absolutely terrified and struggled with her task. My mother suffered from breathing problems after that and until she died, which she attributed to the chemicals.

The Allied bombing strategy was to first drop high explosives, shatter the windows and doors, then drop phosphorus incendiaries to set fire to the city and homes. This, with the favourable weather, created a firestorm. It has been recorded that people and children fleeing from their homes were being "sucked up" by the fires into the flames.

Many people thought they would be safe from the bombs by hiding in cellars. They also died, of asphyxiation as the oxygen was sucked out of the cellars by the fire storm.

Casualties in Dresden from the 1300 bombers attacking during the bombing were officially listed as between 25,000 and 45,000 deaths. This occurred in three days. Many consider it to be far worse because of the huge influx of undocumented refugees. Joseph Goebbels, one of Nazi leader Adolf Hitler's closest allies, claimed it was closer to 200,000 deaths.

When compared to the horrific and well-documented Blitz in London, Dresden was far worse. The Blitz occurred from mid-July to the end of October 1940 – only three-and-a-half months. There were approximately 30,000 deaths during the Blitz. People had prepared shelters and the subways, and there were no fire storms.

In Dresden, my 16-year-old aunt was so frightened that she convinced my mother to run away with her. There were no train stations operating there at the time due to the bombing, so they walked to Leipzig, 111 km away and further into Germany. There, they slept under benches at Leipzig Station for three days until they could get a train.

I visited both Dresden and Leipzig in about 2014. Dresden is a beautiful city on the Elbe River in what was East Germany (1949–1990).

A prominent feature of Dresden was the Frauenkirche Cathedral. It had lain as rubble in the courtyard during the entire Russian occupation after the partition of Germany after World War II. It was rebuilt after the reunification of Germany.

This was after the fall of the Berlin wall in 1989. To my surprise, the British Government had paid for the restoration of the cupola in the church, and the family of the lead bomber pilot of the first raid paid for a new iron crucifix to sit on top of the cupola. The original flame-distorted and bent crucifix is still displayed inside the church.

Some of the stonework in Dresden still had black fire marks. I wondered why they hadn't cleaned them off, and then thought again. The people debated after the war if the city should be completely demolished and rebuilt. They decided to resurrect the original city. The decision to restore the old city kept some of the fire-blackened stones, possibly as a reminder of the past and a as metaphor for Christianity: beauty (life) – utter destruction – redemption.

I, of course, had to visit the train station in Leipzig. I don't know if it had either not been destroyed or been beautifully restored. It had certainly been renovated to accommodate the many stores in the basement. In particular, I looked for the benches. They looked new. I was, selfishly, a bit disappointed.

Back in 1945, my mother and aunt caught the overcrowded train, full of refugees fleeing from Leipzig. The train was crowded with unwashed, lice-ridden refugees, now Displaced Persons (DPs).

It was still very cold and the windows were kept closed. The stench was horrendous in a confined space. This was also a very dangerous trip as the rail lines, stations, interchanges, bridges and trains, if not already destroyed, were prime targets for the Allies' fighter bombers.

My mother and aunt eventually arrived safely in a mainly Latvian DP camp near Oldenburg in Germany. This is where I would later be born.

On entering the camp, a soldier asked if they were the Dombrovskis sisters. They were absolutely terrified, and Mum said it was very difficult not to wet themselves. The soldier was Latvian and he was told by my grandfather, who was already in the camp, to look out for them. There, they were reunited with their parents.

Displaced Camps were hurriedly prepared for the influx of refugees, with the limited material available. Infrastructure like roads, bridges, rail lines, ports and services had been destroyed or damaged due to the war. The delivery of food, fuel and building materials was a real challenge.

Male labour-like tradesmen were also scarce, as many men had been killed or wounded during the war or in prisoner-of-war (POW) camps. Approximately five million German men had died during the war. If one sees pictures of the clean up after the war, one will notice it is mainly done by women and old men.

There were about 10 million DPs in Germany from many different countries just after the war. Our camp was very basic as it previously housed Polish POWs. This indicates that the facilities and comforts were minimal. Now it housed DPs, which included ex-POWs, concentration camp victims, and migrant workers who had been forcibly brought from "home" to work in the factories.

When my mother an aunt arrived in the camp, they had to remove all their clothes. They were sprayed with dichloro-diphenyl-trichloroethane (DDT) and then had to run naked across an open courtyard to the showers. After showering, they were given clean second-hand clothes to wear, donated by various charities. My mother a few times jokingly mentioned that toilet paper was so scarce and rationed it was limited to a single sheet per person, per sitting.

The DP camp was full of traumatised, neurotic, confused, desperate people. Although this camp housed mainly Latvians, there were people from all over Eastern Europe, all speaking different languages and broken German.

The country was lawless, as administrators and police had "disappeared". There was disease and malnutrition, and the black market was rampant. Many were desperate to find family or friends. Some expected to go "home" when hostilities ceased. Some felt so helpless they took their own lives.

Many had survived only by nefarious means and their wits. Many had also disguised their original identity and past to avoid being sent back to the Soviet Union. The Yalta Agreement was that people who were in the Russian Zone before World War II were to be returned "home".

I know of one Ukrainian man who I suspected married a Latvian girl and got her pregnant just so he could avoid being sent back to Ukraine. His son's name was Ukrainian and his mother's Latvian.

The DP camp wasn't safe for single young women. My 16-year-old aunt was sent to England for her safety. It wasn't so altruistic as it at first seemed. They were colloquially called the "white cygnets".

Housing had been a major problem in Britain before World War II. This was further exacerbated in England by the bombing during World War II. Britain was still on war-time rations.

Many people lived in squalid surroundings, sharing the same house, bedrooms and very basic bathrooms. Toilets were outside and shared by several houses. Pollution was rampant. According to my aunt, the conditions were absolutely appalling.

These young girls had to earn their keep and were recruited to do menial tasks like domestic duties and work that no English people wanted to do. Many were exploited and underpaid, if paid at all.

In 2024, I visited the DP camp near where I was born with my cousin near Oldenburg. I expected to find a well-cared for park with trees and flowers to commemorate the people who went through there. Instead, the buildings had been removed or had fallen down. The mess halls and/or washing facilities only had the brick end walls standing. The roofs of these buildings were made from a timber frame and covered with what looked like Sisalkraft (a waterproof fabric made from paper, glass fibre and bitumen). They were dilapidated and some had partly fallen in.

The cobblestone roads were still there. There was long grass and weeds everywhere, and a solar farm now dominated the site. The fence and gate with barbed wire were still there, as were cameras and signs saying "VERBOTEN", which means "forbidden". I was a bit sad as I selfishly expected more to commemorate those that were saved by the camp being there.

On our way out, there was a two metre-high dilapidated black wooden statue of a lady with downcast eyes, holding a small child in her arms. There also was a small plaque telling what this place originally once was.

My father

My father, Arvids, said to me many times that the Germans say: "The hottest fire makes the strongest steel."

He said that the food in the DP camp near Oldenburg was very basic. It allegedly provided about 2,000 calories per day. My father said that most times it was corn soup. His belly was full, but the soup was difficult to digest and seemed to have very little nutrition. My father said he was always hungry. He once told me, after I said I was hungry: "You don't know what real hunger is."

As well as being in the Latvian Army before the war, my father had qualified as a motor mechanic. He was tasked with maintaining the temporary electricity generators that powered the camp.

Before moving into the camp, my father had had a horrific war. He had been a night bomber pilot targeting the Russians. My father and his brother, Verners, were in the Latvian Army, Air Force branch before World War II. They had both graduated as motor mechanics. The photograph of them, in the gallery section of this book, was taken in the 1930s when motor vehicles were considered high tech and needed constant maintenance, and other work was scarce.

The plane's insignia has been blacked out.

It originally featured the Latvian insignia, which was a maroon swastika on a white background. It symbolised "ugunskrusts" (fire cross) and "perkonkruts" (thunder cross) from Latvian folklore. The insignia was used from about 1920 with the formation of the

Latvian Air Force. The Air Force was made up of originally captured German planes left in Latvia after the War of Independence.

The pilot wings were an eagle carrying a red swastika on a chain. My uncle still had his and showed me his original wings.

He told me that the Latvian swastika was changed to a red star in 1940 when he was drafted into the Russian Air Force. Then, the eagle with the red star was changed again to carry the black swastika when the Germans conscripted him in 1943.

The word "swastika" is an ancient Sanskrit word, in use for thousands of years before the Nazis ever adopted it. The Nan Tien Buddhist temple in Wollongong features a Buddha wearing a swastika. The Finnish Air Force only ceased using the swastika in its emblem in 2017.

In June 1940, the Russians occupied Latvia. This was agreed between Germany's Joachim von Ribbentrop and Russian Vyacheslav Molotov. After invasion, the Russians disbanded the Latvian Army.

Many people whom the Russians considered a potential threat were taken into the forest and never came back. My father's cousin, a Captain Vidins who was a career soldier, was "taken into the forest", among others.

The Russians then redrafted the people they thought they could manage and coerced them into their army. Their options were to either join up or be taken for a "walk in the forest". My father took the option of being conscripted into the Russian Air Force. He told me that most of the training he received was in Marxist or communist theory and not much flying.

In June 1941, the Russians rounded up about 15,000 people they considered may be a "problem", or "enemies of the people". These were what some people would call the middle class and above, i.e., public servants, teachers and anyone who could potentially disagree with their doctrine.

They came in the middle of the night, gave them a few hours to pack what they considered essentials and could carry, and deported them to Siberia. The Germans then came in with the start of Operation Barbarossa shortly after in June 1941.

Some Latvians who had been indoctrinated and believed in the Russian propaganda fled with the Russians. Those who didn't remained in Latvia. Some who had seen the Russian atrocities during the occupation considered the Germans "saviours".

Ancient history

Although Latvians were considered "Aryan" (superior race) by Germans, they were not trusted because they had openly resented the original Baltic German landholders. These landholders had seized their land during medieval times and had made most Latvians serfs.

The serfs were not allowed to leave the estate they were assigned to, have a surname, or marry whom they wished.

The Baltic people were the last Pagans in Europe. The land was flat and heavily forested, and there were many swamps. Travel around the area was difficult.

The transformation from Paganism into Christianity was rather complex. The Christian Church was split into the Catholic Church and the Eastern Orthodox Church during the Great Schism in 1054. Genghis Khan began invading from the east in the 1200s. Many Russians and clergy were fleeing west as a result. The Pope in Rome was concerned that the Russians would convert the Pagans in the Baltic to the Orthodox version of Christianity.

The Crusaders had been defeated in Acre in 1291 by the Mamluks (a powerful Muslim military elite), ending their presence in the Holy Land. The Crusaders were becoming a real problem when they got back "home". They had spent a great deal of their fortune to equip themselves to fight this war. They needed horses, armour, weapons, food for the journey, and attendants. They also thought they would replenish their fortunes and add to them with plunder. After the defeat, many were in deep debt.

The Pope sent many of these Crusaders (The Northern Crusaders, Brothers of the Sword, and Teutonic Knights) to the Baltic to convert the Baltic Pagans to the Roman version of Christianity.

Before the Crusaders arrived, the Latvians tolerated these strange people in Riga when they confined their religious practices among themselves. However, when they tried to force these new religious practices on locals, they faced opposition and retaliation.

Many battles were fought, and bishops, priests, monks and knights were killed. One bishop had his head mounted on a stick and was paraded around in the town he was in.

Eventually, the battle-hardened Teutonic Knights, with their superior equipment and experience in the Holy Land, prevailed.

The priests that came to convert the Pagans referred to a book, the Bible, written in Latin, as their authority. At the time, books were hand-written, rare and expensive. This was before the printing press was invented over 200 years later in 1450.

Before this time, the Bible had been verbally translated into one of the six Germanic languages that existed at the time and had to be re-translated and preached in one of the four Latvian languages. (The main Latvian languages at the time were Latgalian, Curonian, Selonian and Semigallian.)

Martin Luther translated the Bible into standard High German in about 1534. The first books were translated from the German Lutheran translation into Latvian in 1586. Before that, there was much inconsistency in interpretation.

Even now the Bible has several versions – the St James version, Lutheran version, Ethiopian version, and Mormon "Book of Scriptures" spring to mind.

This was fraught with many misunderstandings. The people who would unite and become Latvians were taught whatever the priest, who had the authority, interpreted in his own way from his book about a God in Heaven who could not be seen.

The various tribes already knew who their deities were, i.e., the Earth, Sun, Moon, thunder, etc. – tangible things they could see and feel. For these Baltic Pagans, their "church" was not a building but was the Sacred Forest. The Oak (male tree) and the Linden (female tree) were considered sacred.

To "help the Latvians to decide if they wished to convert", the Knights severed a few heads.

Now that the Latvians were baptised into Christianity, they had to pay taxes to support the clergy, for the knights, castles, church buildings, etc. The Latvians before that time only grew in the fields what they needed for the year, hunted and fished. There was minimal surplus.

The Germans brought in "managers" who would help the "locals" produce a surplus so they could pay taxes. They took the land that had been managed and owned for centuries by the local people and made them into serfs. They were forced to relinquish old customs and traditions that the priests considered Pagan.

There were two stories, below, that survived that my mother told me regarding the power of the Moon. The Moon in Latvian mythology is the guardian of men and boys. Mēness (moon) lends his light and protection to those who have to work and travel by night.

There were two young men that left home to make their fortune.

They decided to go separate ways, but before they departed they agreed to meet in a particular place at a certain time a few years later, before going back home.

They made their fortunes and met as arranged. One said to the other in conversation: "We are alone and if I kill you and take your money, no one will know."

The other said, looking up at the sky: "The Moon will see and it will tell."

The first one scoffed and killed his friend and went home a very rich man. He married the most beautiful girl in town, who was originally his friend's fiancé, and was happy.

One evening, he and his wife were walking together hand in hand under a full moon. The young man looked up across his shoulder and said to himself in a barely audible voice: "You can't tell anyone anything." His wife asked what he meant. He replied nothing. She continually pestered him, and eventually he told her. She reported him and he was thrown in jail for the rest of his life.

He could see the Moon through his jail cell bars and it mocked him each night until he died.

• • •

There was a fisherman who was caught in a storm in the Baltic Sea and became shipwrecked on the coast of Sweden. He was saved and brought back to health by a young maiden. When he recovered, he felt he had to return home to tell his parents he was alive and well, so he left her.

The young maiden told him he could return; all he had to do was walk on Moon's light on the ocean. He could easily do this but he must have real faith.

After a while at home, he missed the young maiden and felt he had to go back to be with her. One night on a full moon, he saw the Moon's trail on the water and was beckoned to try to walk on it. He remembered that he must have faith, but hesitated to start the journey. He stepped on the Moon's trail, and to his surprise it supported him. He was very hesitant and slow at first.

He walked for hours, then began to run. Daylight was coming and the Moon's trail started fading. He ran faster and faster. Daylight came, and he could see the shore but it was still a long way off. He sank into the sea and drowned.

If he had trusted what the young maiden had said and was less hesitant, he would have reached the shore alive.

The next day, they found a dead stranger's body on the beach.

The Chinese also have stories of the Moon. Various versions exist in Asia. One is the image on the full Moon depicting a lady, a willow tree and a rabbit.

The rabbit met an old man and sacrificed his own body to feed the hungry man. The man was actually a God in disguise, and for his sacrifice made the rabbit immortal and sent him to the Moon.

An elixir was made by the Jade, or golden rabbit on the Moon. The lady "Chang'e" obtained a bottle, drank the elixir of immortality and floated up to the Moon.

The Chinese celebrate this event with Moon Cakes. I think it's a better story than just the man in the Moon Westerners see.

There are still many ancient Latvian stories. When I was young, my uncle sent me a book of these stories. On the cover he had fashioned my name in silver. I still have this piece of fashioned silver, but I don't know what happened to the book.

The irony of Latvian festivals is that two of the main Pagan festivals have been retained. They have, however, been "rebranded". The two are St John's Day and Christmas Day:

- St. John's Day was originally the Summer Solstice "Jani "or "Ligo" svetki. It was celebrated by young people singing, lighting and jumping over fires, and jumping into the river naked. Some of the younger people would then go into the forest to "look for Fern Flowers". The Summer Solstice was the ideal time to conceive as the baby would arrive in spring, i.e., March, when the weather became warmer.

- The other festival was the Winter Solstice, when small pine trees would be cut down, decorated with small apples, gingerbread and coloured pine cones, and lit with candles. People would dance around it, singing.

  When challenged by the priest for enacting this apparent Pagan festival, their response was: "It's a Christmas tree to celebrate the birth of Christ." This spread to Germany, England and the rest of the world.

Christmas Day is a different day for the Orthodox Christians to the Roman Christians.

A young boy of mixed Greek and English heritage told me he enjoys having the two Christmases as he gets two sets of presents.

Most people don't know that the Christmas tree has its Pagan roots in Latvia. The man in Latvia giving out presents on Christmas Eve wears white clothes and is called "Ziemassvētku vecītis". He represents Yule, the birth of Sun God Mithras. He grows as the days get longer. The man in the red suit is an American invention, used by the Coca-Cola Company in the 1930s to increase sales of their beverage in winter.

The languages and many of the ancient customs were destroyed by Christianity.

My father's ancestors were considered Curonian nobility and had certain privileges. After a truce with the Tectonic Knights, they were initially allowed to retain their name and language and keep their land, but could not employ any labour. They could marry whom they wished and could hunt in the Sacred Forests and fish in the streams. However, they had to "volunteer" to fight a war when required if the German Lord of the area needed them. They also had their own royal crest.

Many palatial houses were built by the Baltic Germans on the hard work of the people they had made into serfs.

There were many invasions by Swedes, Danes and Russians, but the Baltic German landlords retained their influence and power.

Latvia and Germany

The Latvians had no love of the Germans, especially the Baltic Germans.

During the riots that started in Leningrad in 1905, after the defeat of the Russian Navy by the Japanese, the people in St Petersburg rioted. Latvians also rioted and burnt down over 400 Baltic German manor houses as a result. The Latvians also fought against the Germans in the first World War.

Latvians were not trusted by the Germans. I remember my mother singing disparaging songs about the Baltic Germans as nursery rhymes. I was a bit offended by these songs when very young as I was born in Germany.

After the losses in the battles of Stalingrad and Kursk, and the deployment of German troops into Italy after the Italians surrendered, the Germans needed replacement manpower urgently to replace those "lost". The option was given to the Latvians and Estonians to either join the German armed services or go to Germany to work as slave labour in the factories. Lithuanians were not conscripted as the Germans considered them a bit Slavic.

The factories at that time were being heavily bombed by the allies. By joining the armed services, the Germans claimed the Latvians can help fight our "common enemy", the Russians, and perhaps regain our independence after the war. With these options, my father signed up to join the Luftwaffe.

There is an old proverb that says: "The enemy of my enemy must be my friend." The choice of who you wanted to be your "friend" was made by choosing between the communists (whom the English and Americans affectionately called "Uncle Joe") or Adolf Hitler.

Latvia had a horrendous early-half of the nineteenth century. Here are the main events:

- There were the uprisings in 1905 against the Tsar of Russia and the Baltic Germans.
- The Latvian division of the Tsarist army was not supported by the Tsarist commanders when they, as a unit, beat the German Army when they were fighting for the Tsar in the Christmas Battles in 1916.
- Riga was occupied by the Bolsheviks at the end of World War I.
- There was alleged support by the Germans who helped defeat the Bolsheviks.
- The Germans turned on the Latvians when they suspected they wanted independence.
- Poland and Estonia defeated the Germans and Russians.
- The war of liberation lasted from the end of World War I to 1920.
- The confiscation and redistribution of the land occupied by the Baltic Germans was being transferred to the freedom fighters. The Baltic Germans did not want to surrender the land easily.
- The redistributed land after independence was confiscated by the Russians during the first occupation in 1940. The landholders or people who were perceived as a threat to the communists were persecuted.

People tend to easily judge, but if you were faced with the same decision, which decision would you have made when the Germans returned?

After peace was declared, General Patton, commander of the United States Third Army, said: "We have defeated the wrong enemy." Patton had predicted the Cold War. He wanted to use the German Army, together with the United States Army, to go all the way to Moscow.

Before my father left home for war against the Russians, his mother told him: "You will be safe as the only thing that will kill you will be a bullet made of pure gold."

The commander in charge of the squadron was a German officer. All Latvians were subordinate to him.

Part of my father's operations was to fly over the city in a German Arado Ar 66 light bomber plane. This was the city where he had left his wife and baby son before he was drafted into the Luftwaffe. He had also left his parents and friends there.

Many times at night he saw his city of Jelgava, which was the capital of Curonian State and the second largest city in Latvia, in flames. He told me many times: "You can't believe how fiercely a fire can burn in a city." At the time, I didn't appreciate what my father was telling me. He told me many small things that I didn't connect at the time.

Jelgava was on the river Daugava. The Russians were on one side of the river and Germans on the other. They were shelling each other. The Battle of Jelgava in 1944 was reported to be one of the heaviest battles in Latvia, and the city was almost completely destroyed.

My father had flown over his city several times a night. Once, he was ordered by the Germans to bomb positions in his own city. He didn't want to obey the order, but he also couldn't fly back with a load of bombs. He chose to drop his bombs on the Russian side of the river, in the forest, and by chance managed to hit a large Russian ammunition dump.

He told me many times that I couldn't imagine how fiercely an ammunition stockpile can explode. He said it exploded and burnt for three days and nights.

He also told me many times that I need to trust reason over intuition. He didn't have a navigator in the aeroplane. It was dark, and sometimes, flying over strange country, he relied on maps and memory only. He said he knew when he was flying over Russia as the remaining homes had thatched roofs and reflected the light differently.

On one of his first night flights, he took off and saw the Moon behind him. He thought this was good as all he had to do is fly back towards the Moon to get back to the airfield. On his way back, his cockpit instruments were directing him one way but the Moon indicated that was incorrect. He couldn't find his airfield, and then realised he was lost. He was low on fuel, so he searched for a road and landed. After landing, he realised that the Moon moves and that his intuition had overruled his reason.

The Germans wondered how the British could see so well at night; they were unaware of the advances in radar. Spies were told that the British ate a lot of carrots which improved their eyesight. The eye contains carotene, so the explanation seemed reasonable. Night fighters and bombers in the Luftwaffe were prescribed eating plenty of carrots. According to my father, one of his mates ate so many carrots that his body developed an orange tinge.

Being on the Russian front in winter had many challenges. Any engines, including aeroplane engines, wouldn't start because the oil became too thick from the cold when it was not running, and the engine had to be warmed up before it could be started. This became a major problem if the Russians advanced and they couldn't start the engines. The planes would then be destroyed on the ground like "sitting ducks".

Some of the German fighter plane squadrons were issued with electric blankets to cover the engines and keep them warm overnight. There weren't enough electric blankets for all the planes, so my father suggested pouring petrol into the oil to thin it out before the engine went cold. When the engine started and warmed, the petrol evaporated and the oil regained its consistency.

When investigating the problem, the designer of the engines was horrified. However, he was overruled as it was better that the engine was partially compromised for a short while than having the plane sit on the airfield, unable to take off, and subsequently destroyed on the ground.

Another issue was that the brake fluid would freeze during flights and the brakes would not work on landing. The planes would often overshoot the runway and break their undercarriage on landing. At one airport, there was a ditch at the end of the runway. Several of the pilots, who had found their target and had survived the searchlights and being shot at, crashed into the ditch when landing. I believe at least one pilot was killed and several injured.

When the Russians had originally retreated, they had a "scorched earth" policy and would set fire to anything that could be of value to the enemy. When the Germans moved forward, there would be no shelter.

Roads in Russia were unpaved, and when rain came before winter, the roads would turn into quagmires. It was difficult to supply food, fuel, ammunition and spare parts to the front line army.

Much of the food was "ersatz", i.e., artificially manufactured. Coffee was made from roasted barley, acorns or chicory. Bread was usually a "kriegsbrot" (war bread), which had varying, and later increasing, amounts of sawdust as a substitute for flour when it became scarcer.

Railways were of a different gauge, and the Russians destroyed their locomotives which they couldn't take with them. Germans couldn't use their own trains on the Russian train lines.

German weapons were manufactured with a high degree of precision. However, according to my father, Russian weapons rattled but would still fire when frozen in temperatures below minus 20 °C, but the German weapons would seize up when it got cold.

It was so cold that the pilots were issued with electric-heated flying suits that plugged into the plane's electric system and would activate when the engine started. During the day, it was still very cold and the issued uniforms were insufficient. My father would layer his body with newspapers while putting on his clothes to keep warm.

On one occasion, the Germans brought in a truckload of Jewish prisoners to do some manual work on the airfields. They had a bulldozer on the airfield to clear crashed planes, keep the runways clear and pull out planes that overshot the runway.

One of the prisoners was tasked with washing down the muddy bulldozer. It had a petrol engine, and he pulled the electric leads from the distributor to the spark plugs to clean them. He replaced them incorrectly and the engine spluttered when they tried to start it.

The German officer yelled "sabotage" and pulled out his pistol to shoot the prisoner. My father stopped the officer and rearranged the spark plug leads, and the engine started. The prisoner was very frightened. He said something to my father afterwards but my father didn't understand him. Words didn't matter.

They tried to sleep during the day but could hear constant shellfire in the distance. My father said that after one particularly difficult and scary mission, he and a friend decided to go for a drink. This was so they could sleep with the background noise and do it again the next night.

They took a motorcycle with a sidecar and drove to the local bar. When they arrived, my father jammed the brakes and spun the motorcycle. A senior German officer raced out after hearing the noise, pulled his pistol, and put it against my father's head. He yelled: "Do you know how expensive rubber is? Next time you do that, I'll shoot you."

My father was issued with two weapons in case he was shot down: a small machine gun and a pistol. He flew for about 1,200 hours in combat and carried out all his sorties during the night. He was shot down and crash landed three times. He was injured once, and the following evening he would be flying again in another plane.

He told me that he was once caught in a search light, then a second, then a third. The intense, concentrated light would shine through the fabric of his plane and show its skeletal framework. This terrified him.

Everyone within range on the ground was shooting at him, and he knew they all wanted to kill him. This, he said, was very unnerving. My father told me on several occasions that after one particular crash, he landed in "no man's land" in a swamp. When he moved and made a noise, one side would begin shooting, then the other side would retaliate. He crawled out of the swamp, and a tree he was sheltering behind was hit by a shell, demolishing it.

When my father got out of the swamp he was frightened and didn't know which side of the line he was on. He was wet and cold (his electric flying suit was no longer plugged in), and eventually he crawled/walked into an open field. It was still dark and he could hear footsteps following him. He stopped, and quietly said "halt", loud enough to be heard but not to attract attention. The footsteps kept coming. He suspected the person didn't understand German so he must be Russian, so he fired his pistol. The footsteps stopped. He went over and saw he had shot a farmer's cow.

My father then went to the farmhouse, but the people inside wouldn't let him in. He pulled out his pistol and pried it in the gap between the door frame and door, and they reluctantly helped him.

My father told me several times that he was very ashamed of that. He added that he didn't know where he was. It was dark and he was wet and cold and also very frightened.

My father was awarded, among several other medals, the Iron Cross, both first and second class, for his service with the Luftwaffe.

The Latvian pilots were not given the latest and best aircraft – only what could be spared. My father mentioned that his mechanic was Estonian, not Latvian. The Estonian language is very different to Latvian as it has a strong influence from Finland. To converse with his mechanic, my father learnt a bit of Estonian. That little bit once saved his life.

Towards the end of the war, they were ambushed while in their German uniforms by Estonian Partisans. The Latvian Luftwaffe squadrons my father was in were disbanded due to a lack of fuel and spare parts towards the end of the war.

Several Estonian pilots flying for the Luftwaffe defected to Sweden, taking their serviceable planes with them.

My father was transferred to Estonia, which sits just below Finland. The German officers fled the Russian advance leaving behind only non-Germans. On the walk back from the north, my father was the senior Non-Commissioned Officer (NCO) and was put in charge. There was a limited amount of fuel towards the end of the war, so he guided and walked 700 soldiers to a camp in Germany.

After peace, my father and a friend were walking and found an abandoned car. On checking, it had run out of petrol. They had passed by an airfield recently and went back to get petrol. No one was there except a whole lot of brand-new planes just delivered from the factory. My father and his friend punched a hole in the bottom of some of the planes' wings and drained what fuel there was out of them.

They filled and started the car. A high-ranking German officer approached them. He was apparently also fleeing, and at gunpoint took the car. All they could grab was a single bag each.

On another occasion, my father was going somewhere and a jeep with American soldiers stopped and an American officer demanded my father's papers. He pulled out his papers and, from the same pocket, fell a golden star. The officer pointed to the medal on the ground and my father shook his head. He was given back his papers. The officer and the other soldiers pulled out their pistols and indicated that my father should run. He ran as fast as he could while they fired into the air and laughed, and drove away laughing. My father told me that story many times.

According to my uncle, sometimes the Russians could advance as much as 50 km per day.

My uncle Peters (the husband of my mother's sister) was in the German signals division as a truck driver. Each truck had two drivers. The Russians would aim to shoot the driver of the first truck to disable the vehicle and possibly stop all those behind it. After the first driver was shot, the second driver would pull him out of his seat, then take over.

He would jokingly say to my father: "You pilots had it easy, we would have to dig shallow foxholes in the frozen ground and snow at night and try to sleep in them and eat cold rations." He said he would hear an plane engine in the distance and lie awake and strain his ears to its possible direction and location.

Russian harassment bombers ("Nachthexen" or "Night Witches") would fly over, switch their engine off, and swoop down silently and terrorise them every night by dropping bombs. My uncle said you didn't have to be hit to suffer – sleep deprivation did the trick.

One wouldn't know where or if there were any planes coming, as the engines were switched off until the bombs started to fall. My uncle was always alert at night and hoped he had dug his sleeping hole deep enough to protect himself from bombs and shrapnel in the partially frozen ground.

He said to my father: "You pilots would have it easy, as you get up and fly over and terrorise some poor frightened enemy soldiers trying to sleep at night. Then you would fly home, wash, shave and have bacon and eggs for breakfast, and sleep between warm and clean sheets."

My father never responded.

Latvia had lost approximately 30% of its population during the war. This was due to a combination of deportation to Siberia as a result of casualties, or from people fleeing to the American, English or French sectors of Germany. This is proportionally more per capita than Russia lost in World War II.

My father loved flying and always wanted me to be a pilot. When he turned 60, he decided he wanted to get a pilot's licence in Australia. I looked at the instruction book and test and doubted he would pass the theory part. But he did, and he held his licence until his heart problems disqualified him.

The Russians had Commissars in the DP camps in Germany and tried to lure as many Latvians in the camps as they could back to Latvia. Latvia was now in the Russian Zone. My father felt that returning would mean either certain death or deportation to Siberia due to him first being conscripted into the Russian Air Force then changing sides.

He had two options at that time. He could join the Russian Air Force or be suspected as a potential traitor and taken for a "one-way trip into the forest" as many military personnel were. Or he could join the Luftwaffe and fight a common enemy, with the promise of independence when the war is over, or be taken to Germany to work as slave labour in the factories. Even captured Russians who went to work in German factories were considered traitors and either shot or sent to Siberia.

His fear was not imagined, but real. In 1949, just after World War II, his brother and two sisters, who had not left Latvia, were sent to Siberia as part of operation "Priboi". My father never saw them again until I took him back to Latvia, for the first and last time, in December 1991.

The Russians considered those Russians who had been captured and conscripted as slave labour in the factories in Germany as traitors. Many were sent to Siberia after the war.

Stalin said there is no such thing as a Russian POW, just traitors. Many that were released before the end of hostilities were sent straight back into the front line. Senior Russian officers who had surrendered were shot by Russians after being repatriated.

Lithuanians, Latvians and Estonians who stayed behind formed partisan groups after the war to fight the Russians from the forests. The called themselves "mezabrali", which is Latvian for "Forest Brothers". One only came out of hiding in 1991 when Latvia regained independence.

The partisans were supplied by the British to help stem communism. They were operational until about 1956 when they were betrayed by the British aristocrat and Russian spy Kim Philby – a member of the notorious "Cambridge Five".

My father thought, because of what he had seen while flying over Jelgava, that all those he loved or were his friends were most likely dead. He believed nobody could have survived that inferno.

My traumatised father met my mother in the Oldenburg DP camp. He was instantly charmed by her, and also concerned for her safety. I don't know exactly when my mother arrived in the Oldenburg camp, but I suspect, considering the Bombing of Dresden in late February and her walk to Leipzig and then train to Germany, as well as the fact that the camp in Oldenburg still housed Polish POWs until after the end of WWII, it was in the summer of 1945.

I heard the town of Fallingbostel mentioned a few times, where apparently there was a large army barracks and later a DP camp. I suspect it may have been an interim camp.

It was highly advisable for women to have a protector in Oldenburg camp. My mother was physically very attractive at 18 years of age. She had a forceful personality up to the day she died. She was hardly ever "politically correct", and always confidently said what she believed. She was never timid. Some people who didn't know her well feared her. She believed it was better to be proactive and to decide what you want rather than have something imposed upon you.

According to my mother, women who were young, attractive and unattached quickly looked for a man they believed would protect and look after them in the camp.

My father was born in 1914 and my mother in 1926, so he was 12 years older than her.

What she said caught her eye in the camp was that he was reasonably well-dressed and reasonably well-groomed compared to the rest of the men in the camp. He didn't have a limb missing, and he also had "manicured fingernails".

My mother's wedding ring was made from a five lati silver coin in the camp. I was born in a hospital near the camp in May 1946. My father made a pram for me from the only metal available – aluminum and scrap steel from crashed aeroplanes.

Australia

In the wake of World War I, Australia had a concern, echoed by then Prime Minister Billy Hughes: "Populate or perish". Years later, this mantra was repeated by Australia's first Immigration Minister Arthur Calwell after World War II. He wanted more "British white Australians" to come to Australia.

The Japanese in the Pacific frightened the people already living here in Australia. The HMS Prince of Wales, a new battleship, was launched on 3 May 1939. In late 1941, she and the battle cruiser HMS Repulse were sent to protect British eastern possessions, and Australia against Japanese expansion.

Both ships were sunk off the coast of Malaya and Singapore by Japanese land-based bombers and torpedo bombers on 10 December 1941. The so-called "impregnable fortress" and naval base in Singapore was captured by the Japanese in February 1942. The Japanese also bombed Darwin in February 1942 and Broome in March 1942. The Australian Government tried to kept this a secret at the time.

The Japanese had sunk nine ships in Darwin Harbour and two outside the harbour. They destroyed 30 planes in Darwin and killed more than 235 people and wounded approximately 400. In Broome, they killed 88 civilian and military personnel and destroyed 24 aircraft.

When I was visiting Darwin Harbour in 1996, a tour guide told me: "We sold scrap and pig iron to the Japanese before the war. They made bombs from it and came back and sunk our ships. They then got the contract to clear the harbour of shipwrecks after the war. They melted the scrap down again and made Toyotas, which we now buy. Now that's what I call real recycling."

The Japanese shelled Sydney and Newcastle from a submarine in June 1942. Three midget submarines entered Sydney Harbour and sank a naval depot ship, HMAS Kattabul. Twenty-one sailors were killed and 10 were wounded.

In May 1942, there was a major battle in the Coral Sea. This left the Japanese fleet carrier Shokaku damaged, the United States fleet carrier Yorktown damaged, and the USS Lexington so badly damaged it was later scuttled. There were many other smaller ships sunk and/or damaged.

The Japanese occupied islands in the Pacific and landed in Papua New Guinea and Timor.

The hospital ship Centaur was sunk off Brisbane by a submarine, with the death of 268 people.

Thirty-eight ships were sunk around Australia's coastline by the Japanese.

There was also the "Cowra Breakout" where 1,104 Japanese POWs escaped from detention. This was the largest prison escape of World War II.

Approximately 12,000 people of German, Italian and Japanese heritage, among them some who had been naturalised or born in Australia, were interned in Australia during World War II. Australia also interned Jewish refugees fleeing Europe.

In 1945, Australia had a population of only just over seven million.

There was a plan in place to demolish Newcastle steelworks and other industries around Newcastle if the Japanese invaded. There were many bunkers and gun emplacements built around the east coast of Australia.

After the war, there was unrest in countries surrounding Australia. This happened in Africa, Ceylon, India, China, Malaya, Singapore and Indonesia. Some people in Australia thought the unrest could spread to Australia.

Australia first tried to increase its population by bringing in British migrants, many of whom arrived on converted troop Liberty ships. The third-largest component of the Australian population before World War I was of German heritage.

There were problems with Greeks who came to Australia after Turkey had occupied some portions of Greece, and with Italians who fled Mussolini after World War I. They were not considered quite "white enough". They were shunned and, as a result, considered a bit insular.

There were also sectarian conflicts between Catholic descendants of Irish people and English Protestant descendants (often referred to as "WASPs") who had been in Australia for generations.

Australia had a few very large projects that had been on hold, including the Snowy River Scheme and Warragamba Dam. Warragamba Dam was required to increase Sydney's water supply for over 20 years. The delay of these projects was due to the Great Depression and World War II. There were also many smaller infrastructure projects, such as roads, railway lines and bridges that needed repair.

There was also an acute housing shortage at the time. Bricks had to be made and homes built. Towns and cities had to be constructed.

The birth rate in Australia had been very low between the wars and during the Great Depression. Australia needed a vast labour force, eager to work on manual tasks. Australia tried, but could not fill the quota with British people.

Arthur Calwell next selected non-British refugees who looked like the people already in Australia and compiled with the White Australia policy.

The first people who were reluctantly or cautiously approved to come to Australia were from the Baltic countries. There were concerns that another ethnic influx would fracture Australian society even more. Australia didn't want people who could be regarded as "the refuse of war" – old people or those with limbs missing, etc. It was not charity or compassion but pure pragmatism.

Calwell chose young, healthy, good-looking people from the Baltic countries in the first few batches of immigrants.

These were new arrivals who were to be readily accepted to provide labour to build the colony.

My parents, Olga and Arvids Vidins, fitted into the "beautiful Balts" category and were among the first to arrive in Australia, along with two-year-old me.

For publicity, and to show what these DPs looked like, Calwell diverted the DP ship Fairstar to Freemantle, Western Australia. There was a photo opportunity to kiss the 50,000th DP who arrived in Australia. A seven-year-old Latvian girl, Maira Kalnins, beautifully blonde, was chosen from the Latvian DP camp for this purpose.

My father had originally been given the first option to go to Canada, on the condition that he had to go alone and his family would follow. This was completely unacceptable to him because of his previous experience of leaving his former family in Jelgava.

Australia offered whole-family relocations, so he chose Australia. When other nationalities from Europe arrived, the new non-British migrants would be called "New Australians".

For the three of us to come to Australia, we first had to catch a train from Oldenburg, Germany to Genoa, Italy. There, we boarded the Liberty troop ship, which had been converted into a migrant ship, the Castel Bianco, and chartered by the International Refugee Organization. We were alongside 879 other DPs.

This transportation to Australia is recorded as Australia's "Fifth Fleet". Some disembarked in Freemantle and the rest in Sydney.

I can't remember much of the ocean trip except a large bluish fish jumping out of the water ahead of the ship and a group of black sailors on the ship. I don't know if I was alone at that moment, but in retrospect I imagine I wasn't. The sight of the group of young black sailors frightened me.

We landed in Sydney on 18 November 1948 (Latvian date) or 19 November 1948 (Sydney date). The 18th was Latvia's National Day, so it was very significant to my mother. This was also about six days before the release of Australia's own car, the Holden.

When we landed, my father prayed and asked God: "All I really want from this country is good health."

The only luggage we were allowed to bring was packed into one suitcase each.

Years later, when I travelled overseas for work, I would carry a single suitcase and cabin baggage. I would then have a warm hotel room, a shower, dinner, then bed after I arrived at my destination. This simplicity reminded me of my parents' choices. Carrying everything in a single suitcase to relocate to a new country is very different.

About 20,000 Latvians came to Australia before the Russians stopped the "exodus".

A condition of passage was that my father was contracted to work wherever the Australian Government sent him for two years to repay for our relocation to Australia.

Approximately 170,000 people from DP camps migrated to Australia between 1947 and 1954. They had to be described as young, attractive people who, it was said, "if they lay on Bondi Beach would not be indistinguishable from locals". Old people or people with deformities or war injuries were excluded.

My father was approached many years later while at work in the 1960s by a man with a heavy accent, who apparently knew him. He didn't introduce himself but started talking. He knew my father's history and had information about my father's former family.

According to my father, this man knew things only my father thought he could have known himself. He also knew where we lived and the details of our current family. The man later disappeared and my father never saw him again. It was the height of the Cold War and my father suspected he could only have been a Russian spy.

During morning tea one day, a friend of ours, also of Latvian descent, said that when her father was working inside the steelworks he was approached by a stranger who knew everything about his former life. I told her that my father had a similar experience.

In the 1960s, my father discovered that his first wife and son had survived the war and that his brother and two sisters, who had been deported, had been released from Siberia.

When I saw his first wife's gravestone, it was apparent she had never remarried. My father was traumatised as this technically made him a bigamist.

Although I heard my parents say it was difficult, I never realised how difficult it was to settle down in a new country, with a different language and cultural customs, until I began working overseas in Thailand and China.

I had often asked myself, how can "the heart" that has been hardened in the forge of the furnace of war retain the toughness and still not be embittered, and have sufficient malleability to start again "from scratch" in a new country? This is especially challenging when one is not fully accepted and must learn a new language, new food, customs, traditions and lifestyle.

In 1989, when I was 43 years of age and after the fall of the Berlin Wall, I arranged for my older step-brother, whom my father thought had perished during the war, to come to Australia from Latvia for a visit. It was a very tortuous process to get him here.

His visit was full of mixed emotions for my father. He often repeated: "He's my son but I didn't even know him."

I got a shock when I met him. The way he stood, the way he thought, was very similar to me. Yet he had a different mother, grew up in a completely different environment and country, and received a different education.

My father had no influence in his upbringing. How could this be? This, I reasoned, could not have been learnt independently. Was it genetics? I later found out that people from the Baltic regions have the highest incidence in Europe of hunter-gatherer DNA in their make-up. I had my DNA tested and 31% of it is hunter-gatherer.

DNA has revealed that Latvia and Lithuania have had the least intervention by other migrations, probably because it was cold, swampy, and heavily forested and not very welcoming.

In 1991, I took my parents to Latvia to meet their remaining relatives. My uncle, my father's older brother Verners, who had been sent to Siberia, was now 80 years old. He danced on the table and tried to get me drunk. He sang songs that had been banned by the Russians.

I was amazed by his resilience, especially after the traumas he must have suffered during his time in Siberia.

When my parents and I had arrived in Australia in 1948, we were placed in a camp at Bathurst made up of unlined Nissen huts.

Inside a single Nissen hut similar to the one in Bathurst were several families, separated just by a curtain.

This was a disused army camp built just before World War II. It was "hot as hell" in summer and "cold as charity" in winter. No power outlets for internal heating were allowed. This was refused with the excuse being that the outlet may have been used for cooking.

I can also remember seeing snow on the ground. Washing, toilet and messing facilities were all communal.

The Australian Government had a deliberate policy of putting the DPs in camps that were not suitable for "locals". They didn't want the people already in Australia to think that these DPs were living in "the lap of luxury".

Meals consisted of the specified 2000 calories a day and were cooked in a simple way common at the time and reminiscent of plain, basic British fare. Most people complained, not so much about the food but about the cooking. The meat was stinky and boiled fatty mutton. After that, my father wouldn't eat lamb, having been served it in the camp.

The DPs were not allowed to suggest changing to meals they were familiar with. They were also not allowed to cook food they were familiar with in their homeland. Different ways of cooking, ingredients and cuisines from Europe had not really arrived in Australia at that time.

The exception was in the larger towns and cities where Greeks who arrived fleeing the Turks in the 1920s established "milk bars". Remnants of these milk bars in the Art Deco style are "The Paragon" in Goulburn and Katoomba, New South Wales. They served hamburgers, hot dogs, ice cream sodas and milk shakes. These was copied from American fare.

There were also many Chinese-run restaurants in Australian country towns which served (allegedly) Chinese foods cooked in a different way. They often had a sign in the window, "Australian meals served also". This usually meant steak, eggs and chips. Sometimes, diners would get a bottle of beer from the pub next door to have with their meal.

Delicatessens selling premium food delicacies started to appear in the mid-1950s with German migration. The delightful smell would be the first impression on entering the store. Delicatessens have since deteriorated to become the sanitised "Deli".

Italian food also had a significant impact, initially in the suburb of Carlton, Victoria.

A condition of entry into Australia was that my father had to work wherever the government sent him for a period of two years to repay the cost of our passage to Australia. He was sent to work in Sydney for the Sydney Water Board. This was very far from the Bathurst camp.

He worked in tunnels under Sydney, presumably for the distribution of water from Warragamba Dam. The unions were very active and militant. He told me that on one occasion they had a "stop work" because it was raining outside. They were in a tunnel so they were shielded from the rain, but if the people aboveground stopped work because of rain, those underground had to stop work too in a sign of solidarity.

My father once said he had escaped from the communists and they are here also, in the unions.

My younger brother Rudolfs was born in the Bathurst camp.

Overseas qualifications were not accepted in Australia. It has been said that more than 10% of the DPs were professionals and 300 were medical doctors. All DPs, regardless of experience or qualifications, were classified as labourers (for men) or domestics (for women).

The Australians already here didn't want people that may challenge the "locals" for jobs. They wanted able and willing workers to do manual work that was in demand, or what "locals" didn't want to do.

My father wrote many letters to us while we were in the Bathurst camp. He also drew pictures on the bottom of the letter especially for me. Photos of his letters are in the gallery section.

Bowral

Bowral is a small country town in New South Wales, first settled in the 1840s. The railway was completed in 1867 and the town grew slowly after that. My father arranged to rent a home in Bowral, and my mother and I moved there in February 1950.

The house was one of the oldest remaining homes in Bowral. It was on a one-acre block on the corner of Bowral and Walker Streets. The owner of the house was a Mr Walker, whom the street was named after. The address was 1 Walker Street, one street off and parallel to Bong Bong Street, the main street of Bowral.

The house was very basic, but certainly better than being sent into the forest in Siberia where my father's brother and sisters were sent in 1949. My father's siblings were taken to Siberia at the start of summer and, according to my mother, had to build their own simple shelter with basic hand tools before winter set in a few months later. Otherwise they would have died from lack of a shelter.

My then 18-year-old mother and her 16-year-old sister would have most likely been raped and brutalised by Russian soldiers in 1944 if they had stayed.

The home in Bowral had a large barn or stables built from wooden slabs, with a dirt floor and a laundry (washing facilities) at one end, not far from the main house.

The horse bridles and harnesses were still hanging on one wall. There were gaps between the timber slabs used to make the walls where the slabs had shrunk.

The kitchen was a large building separated from the stables and house. Early colonial kitchens were built separately from the house to keep the heat from the almost constant kitchen fire. The open fire was used to cook meals and make bread. There was always a chance of a kitchen fire spreading to the living quarters, so it was usually separate. There were also the smells and the flies.

The separate kitchen also served to keep convicts or ex-convict servants out of the main living quarters.

The floors, walls and ceiling were made from hand-sawn timber. There was a huge brick fireplace at one end, with a chain hanging from inside the chimney for cooking bread, meat or vegetables. The fire would have to be going most of the time.

The brickworks were established in Bowral in 1920, so the original chimney may have been stone or galvanised iron. This was normal, as I've seen it in several old, abandoned homesteads.

Initially, the kitchen was without electricity, gas or running water. Reticulated water was roughly retrofitted in the 1920s.

The windows were sash windows propped open with stick. There were no fly screens. Flies were a major problem in Australia at the time, most likely because of the large number of domestic and farm animals. Around each town there were several dairy farms.

The Australian Government was concerned about the fly problem. They asked some of Australia's top scientists at the CSIRO to develop something to keep the flies away when Queen Elizabeth II visited Australia in 1954. The CSIRO developed "Aeroguard" for the Queen.

Later, in 1956, a scientist, a refugee from Hungary, saw the fly problem. After a lot of research he introduced the Dung Beetle.

There was no fridge or ice box to keep food cool. Meat was either salted or hung to be dried from the ceiling in a "Coolgardie safe". The walls and ceiling were painted a cream colour and covered with fly "specks".

You could hear rats running and squeaking in the ceiling. To get rid of the rats cavorting in the ceiling, Mum would smash a glass bottle, sieve out the "glass sand" and smash the remainder until it was all like sand. She would mix it with flour and water and leave it for the rats. This might sound gruesome and cruel, but it's how "Wolfram", a common rat poison that kills rats by causing internal bleeding, is made.

The squeaking and running would stop, then would come the smell. While the smell was there it would be followed by the blow flies.

After that, we put up with the rats. The scurrying and noise was better than the smell and the subsequent blow flies.

To cook anything, my mother would have to chop wood, light the fire, and hang a huge cast iron pot over the fire and continually watch it so the food didn't burn and stick to the bottom.

My father made a bench, obtained a huge timber circular cutting saw and an old motorbike engine, and made a belt-driven bench saw. It did the job but was very dangerous and would be totally illegal today.

Later, my father bought my mother a small brass Primus kerosene stove. Lighting it was intricate, and I remember Mum on her hands and knees on the floor crying as she tried to light it. If the pot on top of the stove wasn't constantly watched and stirred, the concentrated direct flame would burn its contents.

Reticulated gas had been roughly retrofitted for gas lights in the kitchen and living quarters in 1889. The pipe work conduits were visible and exposed. When we moved in, the gas was no longer operational.

Electricity had also been retrofitted in 1925, with exposed conduits to a single light fitting in the ceiling and a suspended pull cord to switch it on and off. There were no other electric power outlets. One could use an electrical device by removing the light bulb and plugging it into the light socket.

My parents retrofitted an old, second-hand "Kooka" slow-combustion stove in the space where the original fireplace had been.

To iron clothes, an "iron" was placed on the stove to heat up before use. There was no such thing as an electric steam iron. Mum would take a glass of water, take a sip, and spray it on the clothes before applying the iron.

We eventually bought a kerosene refrigerator. I don't know how it worked, but one filled a container of kerosene under the fridge and lit it.

The bathroom was also retrofitted, I imagine, after reticulated water was connected to the house. There was a large, deep cast iron bath with a wood-fired "chip heater" at one end. It had to be filled with wood chips, then the cold water running through the internal heater pipes would be turned on and the wood chips would be lit. It had no temperature regulation, so the first water was cold and later became very hot. To turn off the heater you had to put the lid on the burner and wait.

The bathroom was large, with weatherboard floor, walls and ceiling. The vertical wall timbers had rotted where they joined the floor so there was a gap, and in winter the cold wind would blow in through the gap.

Mum would struggle with the washing in the stables, where the firewood heated a large "copper boiler" that was in a brick enclosure. Laundry was boiled, and in those days nappies were reusable and made from cloth.

My mother and grandmother made their own soap with the old fat from cooking and caustic soda which was heated and stirred. Sometimes, a bit of copper sulfate was added. It was poured into trays and allowed to cool, then cut into blocks. The debris would float to the top, and it smelt and looked disgusting.

Mum would pull the laundry out of the copper with a big stick and place it in a "mangle" with large-diameter wooden rollers, open gears and a crank handle. Excess water would be squeezed out. The clothes would then be hung to dry on a washing line. The washing line was like two crucifies, with arms pivoting around the centre bolt. These pivoting arms were to make the line hang low enough on one side to hang the washing. The arms would be levelled to raise the washing line. There was usually a forked stick in the centre to prop up the sagging clothesline.

The path from the front gate to the house was made of large, thick pieces of tree bark laid end to end to prevent mud being walked into the house.

We were either the first or among the first DPs in Bowral. Mum had to survive in a very unfamiliar environment, with two young children. There was no support. We had to eat different foods, navigate shopping, and Mum knew a few basic words but didn't have a conversational command of English.

There were a few things I saw that made an impression on me in Bowral in the 1950s that one doesn't see now. It wasn't unusual to see a swagman (or "swaggy" as we called them) walking up Bowral Street. They usually had on a well-worn, dirty suit, apparently the only clothes they had, and were carrying a swag and a "billy" (billy can) or two. They usually had a dog or two for company.

There was one older lady who lived down the road who had a German Shepherd dog. She would give the dog a cane basket and put a note with some money in the basket. The dog would go to the shops alone, and the shopkeeper would pick out the note, take the appropriate amount of money, and put the goods in the basket. Occasionally, the dog would be rewarded by the butcher who would put a bone in the basket. The dog wouldn't eat it until, presumably, he was at home.

The milkman would milk his cows and put the milk in a large container on the back of his small truck or "ute". He'd drive around the streets, and the ladies would run out with their jugs, saucepans and billies. They'd queue up behind the milkman who would pour a measured amount of milk into their containers.

The milk was delivered in the morning on a daily basis. A small bottle of milk was offered to each child at school. On top of the milk floated the cream.

There were many dairy farms in the district. These slowly disappeared after Britain entered the common market.

The greengrocer would drive around with his truck and groceries, and people would go out to him to buy what they needed.

When Mum wanted something really special for Sunday lunch I would go to the chicken coop, catch a chook, chop off its head, hold it in a bucket until it stopped kicking, then pluck and gut it. Next, I had to singe the young feathers off. I never liked the plucking as it would stink. Now, we can order a pre-cooked chook and pick it up or even have it delivered at home.

The iceman would come around and fill our icebox with a large block of ice.

On occasions, I saw two men walking down the main street of Bowral with guns over their shoulders, carrying a three-metre-long curtain rod between them. On this curtain rod would be many dead rabbits hanging upside down by their back legs. I imagine the men would sell them to the butcher.

In addition to flies, Australia had a plague of rabbits in the 1950s. Skinned and gutted rabbits were displayed in the windows of butcher shops with their kidneys exposed. Myxomatosis, a highly infectious and fatal disease for rabbits, had been introduced into Australia in 1950. Infected rabbits would have white spots on their kidneys. From memory, the rabbits were four shillings a pair.

When my mother went shopping, the labels stating what was in the containers or packages were written exclusively in English. Barlow's, the grocery store, had a long table or counter, with groceries stacked along the back wall. The proprietor would ask what you wanted, then run up the aisle between the counter and shelves, pick what you asked for and place it in your basket.

He'd wrap some of the goods in a brown sheet of paper and tie the package with string, which was on a roll suspended from the roof. There was a skill in breaking of a piece of string, tying it around a finger and pulling and snapping it.

For my mother, there was a fair degree of pointing to select what was needed.

For cooking, the choices were dripping, lard, copha or butter. Cooking oils arrived with migrants a lot later. In 1950s Australia, olive oil was only available from chemists as a cure for earache.

Australians were traditional tea drinkers. Coffee came in later and then it was usually blended with chicory. An alternative was coffee and chicory essence. It came in a square bottle with a picture of a Turkish man wearing a fez on the label. This was prohibitively expensive.

Money was much more complex than the metric system Mum was used to, with ten-pound, five-pound and ten-shilling notes. There were also Guineas, but they were rarely used. There were coins, florin, crowns, one shilling, sixpence, threepence, pennies and half-pennies, or ha'penny, and then weights – pounds and ounces. Everything had to be calculated and written on the brown paper or, if simple, mentally.

There were three pennies to a thrupence and six to a sixpence. There were 12 pennies to a shilling and 20 shillings to a pound. Then there were 16 ounces to a pound. The one pound in weight wasn't the same as one pound in money.

I'd challenge anyone now to simply and accurately convert dollars and cents to pounds, shillings and pence, and to convert the different weights, especially while learning a new foreign language at the same time.

The butchers was even more challenging. They had most of the meat hanging on a rail on hooks behind the counter. They had large-diameter tree stumps about one-metre high standing upright behind the counter. They used the stump as a work bench for cutting and chopping. When you wanted meat, the butcher would select a piece from the hook and then cut or chop it. He'd also trim off any fat if requested. The floor was covered in a layer of sawdust.

On very special occasions, Mum would ask me to go to the butcher to get a half-pound of rum (rump) steak. The next part was complex. I remember it cost five shillings a pound. The piece cut was an estimate of the weight and had to be weighed to confirm it.

If it was only seven ounces instead of eight (half-a-pound), the maths was five shillings (i.e., 12 pence per shilling, seven ounces of 16 ounces in a pound). The cost was $(7/16) \times (5 \times 12)$ equals 26 pence + (2/8) pence (i.e., rounded off to two shillings two pence). This would be described as "two and tuppence".

It wasn't uncommon for people to pull out of their pocket or purse a handful of different coins and show it to the provider of the goods. They trusted the grocer or butcher to pick out the correct amount.

If you wanted two or more items it got even more complicated. Minced meat was easy as the butcher could add or subtract weight by taking a bit off or adding a bit. The cost was worked out and penciled on the inside of the wrapping paper. Butchers and grocers always had a pencil behind the ear. There were no calculators – just cumbersome adding machines, which shops never used or even had.

As a child, I had to learn my maths quickly or be vulnerable. The measurement system was also complex – inches, feet, yards, acres, miles and knots.

It would have been as easy to us now if we would have to do our maths with Roman numerals. What does MMXXV–MCMXCE equal? Or what does C x VI equal?

Mum often mentioned having difficulties with the language, and I thought I understood, but 50 years later I realised what she really meant. While I was working in Bangkok I visited a large Thai restaurant. I was the only foreigner or "ferung" there and I had to go to the bathroom.

The signs were all in Thai and there was no picture indicating toilets. In Australia, most toilets have a picture of either a man or woman on the door or wall.

I watched where people "went", but nobody seemed to "want to go". And I couldn't gesticulate what I wanted without being arrested.

In China, when I went to a restaurant, where I normally would go to eat by myself, I would draw a chicken, fish or pig on a serviette. The staff tried to hide their giggles but they brought me roughly what I wanted. What could I draw on a serviette to the waitress in Thailand to ask for a toilet?

Sometimes, like the toilet in Russia's international airport, one can smell it. This Thai restaurant was very clean. I thought I was about to "pee" in my pants.

In my next Thai lesson I asked how to say toilet. 'Hong Nam'. I don't think it's a phrase I'll ever forget.

Thai is a tonal language – the same word with a different tone can mean the opposite. For example, the word "beautiful" with a different tone can also mean ugly. My hearing is damaged, and I suspect I may also be tone deaf as I couldn't distinguish different tones.

One cannot fully understand what some words means until they have fully experienced the word. My daughter, when she was 16 years old and had found a boyfriend, sat on the steps one evening and said to me: "Dad, you don't really know what love is." I looked at her and said: "How do you think you got here?"

A woman can't explain to a man fully what the experience of childbirth is like. One can hear the words, think they understand the meaning of what is said, but can't really comprehend it.

When we arrived in Australia, even though we were white and looked similar to the locals, we were classified as "aliens" and were treated accordingly by most locals. My parents moved from Walker Street soon after my mother's parents, Janis (John) and Maria, and my aunt Helena and uncle Peters arrived in Australia.

My father rented a house on Daphne Street, about 1 km out of town. It was about a two-acre property, surrounded on three sides by farmland and on the fourth by a block of units and houses that would be rented out mainly by holiday seekers from Sydney. The house was called "Bella Vista", which in Italian means "beautiful view". In Latvian, "vista" means "chicken".

The house was on a large block which came with a shed. My father, after completing his day job, would carry out repairs and maintenance on cars and small trucks.

Life was tough, and I can remember that many times we just had sauerkraut soup for dinner, sometimes with a diced potato. I remember it well as I really hated it.

We struggled to make ends meet, so Mum rented out a few rooms to the Neumanns, a German couple. They had a son who was a bit older than me. We became good friends. We'd sneak onto a large property and steal a bamboo cane to make fishing rods. He'd make the reels from wood. All we needed was fishing line and hooks. We saved up for that and bought a small reel of nylon fishing line, which we shared.

Mum was amazed at how thrifty the Neumanns were. Nothing was wasted – potatoes would be washed but never peeled ("Felts Kartoffel") and orange skins were cooked with sugar to make a candy.

Mum tended a small veggie patch with potatoes, onions, cucumbers, cabbage and radishes. When Mum peeled potatoes, Mrs Newman would be horrified. She'd gather up the thin skins of new potatoes, wash and dry them, then make potato soup. With the thicker, older potato skins, she'd put salt on them and bake them in the oven to crisp up.

Mum reasoned Mrs Newman was from a city in Germany where food was very scarce. Anything edible was gathered and eaten just to survive. Mum said we were from the country and could always grow something to eat.

Mr Newman drove a truck; he purchased it and then purchased another. He modified the newer one so it could carry a larger load without exceeding the road limits.

From what I saw as a child, Mr Newman had been more than a truck driver before he migrated here. I may have come to that conclusion because of his ability to make do with whatever was available. When he didn't have something he wanted, he made it. I also saw that he encouraged his son Klaus to make do with what he had.

I thought Klaus was very clever. When television was introduced, he made a pretend TV set out of a small wooden box, with a window on one side and a story inside on a scroll which would show different pictures as he scrolled. It also had a small TV antenna.

He made all of his toys out of wooden blocks. On Klaus's birthday, his father bought him a small stationary steam engine. You put in the water and fuel, lit it, and it would reciprocate, blowing steam. It had a steam whistle, and Klaus built attachments for it.

I really envied it. In about 1980 I was working in Lismore and bought my son a steam traction engine. It was similar to the stationary steam engine but it moved after it was steamed up and had water and fuel added.

In about 2000, I saw another similar, second-hand steam traction engine in an antique store near Mulwayla where I was building an explosives plant. I immediately bought it, steamed it up, and then played with it. I still have it and think of Klaus every time I look at it.

Klaus even made a functioning tape recorder when he was a young teenager and still going to school.

Unfortunately, to my knowledge, he never married and he died while he was still young.

There was another migrant family that stood out in my eyes living near Bowral. Their name ended with "ich", which indicated possibly Croatian heritage. In the 1950s, both his son and daughter were attending University in Sydney, studying law.

Several others arrived in the Bowral region from different countries, but they all conversed in German. When my parents disagreed with each other about how to discipline me, they spoke German.

I learnt a basic form of German fairly quickly before I started school.

In those days, migrants in Bowral were rare. Instead, we more often saw colourful local characters. On one occasion, a group of rabbit hunters came in with a ute and wanted my father to look at it. They looked, even to me, like men who lived under or close to the truck, never washed or shaved, and used their dogs as a warmer when it got cold at night. The ute looked like it hadn't been cared for and had had a hard life.

One headlight lens/reflector was held in place with a white cotton singlet tied around the bulbous light assembly to keep the lens in. My father got the ute into a drivable condition. When the men had to pay, they didn't have enough money, so they reached a deal and gave my father the ute. They could redeem it when they had the money. They never came back.

During school holidays there was a group of big children (probably in their early teens) who would set up a large army surplus tent on the creek flat below our home in Daphne Street.

They had two greyhound dogs which ran free. When one dog caught a rabbit, they would take it from the dog and skin and gut it. They would give the dog the head and feet and then cook the body on a small stone fireplace with a metal grill on top. They would stay there for days, living on rabbit and a few potatoes cooked in the ashes.

We later bought a home at 40 Bowral Street, near town, in the mid-1950s. The house was "gerry built" just after World War II when there was a shortage of building materials and skilled labour. It had rendered outside walls and the internal walls were an unpainted soft brown wall board. The wall board was so soft you could mark or indent it with a fingernail. The floor was covered with blue felt to cover the rough sawn timber.

We had many parties there for special occasions, and my parents invited the neighbours and people who helped us fit in.

My mother and her sister spent several days cooking special treats like bacon rolls ("pirag"), beetroot salad ("rossel"), potato salad, herring salad and rollmops, borscht, cakes and biscuits, and "zaki ausis", a pastry made of dough, deep fried and shaped like a rabbit's ear and dusted with icing sugar. Italians have something similar, but not the same shape, called "crostili".

She would also buy salted whole herrings in a small, one-gallon-sized wooden barrel, which she had to desalt and prepare. I haven't seen these barrels of salted herrings since the 1950s.

My uncle Peters would catch fish, catch and smoke eels, and shoot rabbits, kangaroo and water fowl. Mum and her sister Helena prepared a real feast with what we caught or could afford to buy. My father didn't participate in these hunting and fishing activities, but he wouldn't discourage me from going with my uncle.

As children, we would "fish" for yabbies. The number we aimed for was the magical 100.

The adults partied very loudly, drank, ate, and sang the old songs they had learnt as children, as well as war songs, both German and Australian. They played the accordion, mouth organ and spoons and danced wildly. I thought that's what everyone did.

Several of the neighbours were invited but didn't come, but the ones that did sat in chairs and watched. I asked myself why they behaved like that. They sat there like "store dummies".

As for my parents, I reasoned that they and the other "refos" had lost everything and many of the people close to them. They were in a strange land and had to adapt. They saw and experienced many horrific things first-hand during the war that the neighbours hadn't.

The "refos" knew and appreciated what it was like being alive and still being physically intact. They celebrated life to the full.

As I grew older I went out and ventured into partying. The major ethnic dances I went to were Latvian, German and Polish. The Germans in the 1960s behaved the same as my parents did earlier – there was wild, noisy music, communal singing, and boisterous eating and drinking.

A friend of mine took me to a Polish dance. They were even wilder, especially when they danced the Polka. I went to several "Aussie" dances in the 1960s. The girls sat on one side of the hall and the boys on the other. To meet a girl, you had to catch her eye and "cross the floor". No eating, drinking or singing.

After my father's two-year contract with the government expired, he found a job closer to Bowral at Gilberts Bus Service in Mittagong. He was employed as a motor mechanic speciaising in diesel engines. Gilberts Bus Service started in Mittagong in 1946, though it doesn't exist anymore.

Dad spoke Latvian, German, a bit of Russian and some broken but understandable English.

A few of the DPs that had arrived in Australia had limited skills suitable for normal life in Australia. Their lack of education was due to the war. They took up truck driving where their command of English was less important.

When trucks needed servicing or repairs, they would come into Gilberts Bus Service. The boss couldn't understand them so he would call my Dad to translate. He always could, and the boss was amazed that Dad could speak to almost anyone from Europe. The boss didn't realise that due to the war, when many countries were occupied by Germany, most people could speak German.

He thought my Dad was more multilingual than he actually was and that he spoke all the European languages. He once asked my Dad: "What language do you think in?"

On a few occasions, what my mother called "rich people" would charter a bus from where my father worked and go down to the beach in the Wollongong area. Some employees and families from the bus depot were also invited. We'd spend the day there, have a picnic lunch, and be driven back home.

There was a dairy farmer whom everyone called Mack or Mr Mack, who was an ex-Barnados boy. He'd been transported to Australia as a 15-year-old and basically had to fend for himself. The Barnados charity took children who had been orphaned or children from vulnerable situations from England, Scotland and Ireland and resettled them in Australia. About 130,000 British children unaccompanied by their parents were transported to Australia between 1920 and 1970. It could be described as possibly the white equivalent of the "Stolen Generations".

His family and mine became very friendly. Everyone in Bowral seemed to know Mack. His daughter Doreen said to me once that she would feel embarrassed when she and her girlfriends walked past a certain pub and would hear her father, with a louder voice than anyone else in the pub, telling stories, usually peppered with swear words. He would say what he thought.

One day, my father was on the farm with him and Mack was about to clean his rifle. Rabbits were in plague proportions then before the introduction of Myxomatosis in the 1950s.

There was a rabbit running in the distance. Mack handed my Dad the rifle and said: "You can't hit that." My Dad reluctantly took the rifle, to be sociable (he normally hated guns), aimed and fired. He hit the running rabbit. Mack exclaimed: "How in the bloody hell did you guys lose the bloody war!"

Mrs Mack, or Noel (she was born on a Christmas Day), was probably a very old-fashioned, traditional Australian lady. When Mum and I visited her she would leave us and put on a record, usually Harry Belafonte or a popular song at the time such as How Much is that Doggy in the Window?

She'd race into the kitchen and mix up a batch of scones and cook them in her modern electric oven. They'd be served with cream and jam and a pot of tea while chatting. I haven't seen anything like that since, except when I was working in Mt Isa in about 2000.

I once visited a farmer with an old surveyor colleague of mine from Papua New Guinea. When his wife saw us she ran into the kitchen and baked a cake to have with tea.

Mack had a small Desoto truck with which he delivered milk in the mornings. Occasionally he'd take us to Wollongong Beach. He'd throw a few hay bales in the back of the tray which we'd sit on and we'd drive down Macquarie Pass singing, with my uncle Peters playing the accordion.

After a while my Dad changed employers with a better offer. He was lucky that he was never out of work. He took up a job in a garage in Moss Vale that serviced and sold British "Standard Vanguard" cars and "Ferguson" tractors. This business also doesn't exist anymore.

School

I started at the local public school in Bowral in the early 1950s with hardly a word of English. I could speak Latvian and German fluently, albeit a child's version. I've lost that ability with my original languages due to lack of use. However, I can still understand specific words, but I don't feel confident with constructing sentences.

I looked and behaved a bit differently to the other children there. I didn't know the rules of cricket, which was almost a mortal sin in the town where Australian cricket hero Don Bradman was born. I was even given a cricket bat, which I never mastered, and would go down to the creek and float it like a boat.

Mum had made all my school clothes. I never had any pocket money like some of the "rich kids" did.

When I learnt some English, I was asked where I was born. I would ask my Mum. She replied that I was born in Germany. The next day when I went to school, I would tell the boy that had asked me that I was born in Germany.

The day after he had spoken to his Dad, who, ill-advised but possibly with the best intentions, told him I was a Nazi. There may have been a bit of ignorance and racism there also.

The next day I was called a "Nazi", and he and other boys would beat me up. I asked my Mum what a Nazi was. She replied they were very bad people. If the boys were right, I thought I must also be a very bad person. Mum said I wasn't.

It wasn't unusual for me to be beaten up and to return home bloody and without buttons on my shirt. I was the only person in my class (maybe school) who was not from Anglo-English or Irish heritage.

I didn't mix readily, mainly because the boys shunned me for being a Nazi. I didn't interact much with them and so didn't learn English quickly. I learnt quickly not to say too much, otherwise I got hurt.

I don't know if the teacher separated me or thought I was dumb due to my lack of English skills and made me repeat kindergarten. The next year, after repeating, I was the tallest in the class.

Daphne Street where we lived was about a mile from school. I had to walk to and from school as we didn't have a car. Even if we had one, Mum couldn't drive. My Dad bought me a 24-inch push bike. I remember it cost 24 pounds. The weekly basic wage at the time for my Dad was 11 pound 16 shillings a week. I think it took at least a year to pay off.

The local Catholic Priest would come around occasionally to see how we were settling in. He had a late-1940s vintage Vauxhall, and my father would service and repair it. When the Priest found out I was having a hard time he suggested I change to a Catholic school. My Dad said he was Lutheran but Mum was Catholic. I was re-baptised Catholic and enrolled in Bowral Catholic School.

The nuns there knew my story and were very sympathetic and helpful. In the early 1950s, sectarianism (Anglicans, Presbyterians, Methodists, Catholics and Freemasons) was still a very bitter issue.

In those days, Catholic schools weren't government-funded. I used to walk to and from school, and the boys from my old school used to wait for me under a bridge. Now I was a Catholic and a traitor as well as a Nazi, so I deserved even more to be bashed up.

I did well in the new school and came second or third in the class. After that, we moved to Wollongong and I went to a new Catholic primary school. There were students from southern Europe but none from the Baltic States or Northern Europe.

There was, however, an exceptionally beautiful girl whose name ended with the letters "en" which I later found out suggested her heritage was Finnish.

Here, the nuns in Wollongong were not as sympathetic as the ones in Bowral. One older nun had a particularly bad experience in China with the communist takeover.

Classes were completely overcrowded. In one class we had 96 pupils taught by one nun. Sister Mary Agnes, who to us was very old, taught all subjects. I've heard comments that the number is very hard to believe.

The era was after World War I, when 38.7% of men between the ages of 18 and 44 had been conscripted, the Great Depression, World War II and the sudden influx of immigrants.

It was the era of the post-war baby boom. The building of schools and training of teachers couldn't keep up. Catholic schools were not government-funded until the late 1960s.

To control some of the boys being disruptive in class, Sister Agnes (we used to call her "Aggie") tried to control all the boys by sitting each of them next to a girl. It worked.

It was rumoured that Aggie was teaching in China before the communist takeover. She and several other nuns had been stripped naked, put on a small boat and pushed out to sea. American sailors found them, clothed them, treated them for exposure, fed them and saved their lives.

There was a particular boy in class from the Island of Volcano of the coast of Sicily. When he received the strap for misbehaviour, he would roll over on the ground screaming and kicking. He'd jump out of the classroom window to avoid getting the strap. It was all theatre. He ended up as a Professor of Education in an Australian university.

It was a different era. There was a mantra repeated at the time by many people as well as the Catholics: "Spare the rod and spoil the child." The nuns carried a thick, wide leather strap. This was more as a deterrent than a weapon.

The nuns and brothers I met were exceptionally dedicated people. Sister Mary Aquino noticed my singing voice and sent me for extra lessons. I can still remember the words to the song:

> Come dressed in your gown in blue brocade, a rose
> upon each dainty shoe.
>
> Soft powdered hair and wistful face, shy dreaming
> eyes of tender blue.
>
> Lady in loveliness array, I'd love to dance with you.

It was a different time then.

I became a contestant in the Wollongong Eisteddfod to represent the school. I came third in the area, which went west as far as Goulburn.

The next year my voice broke.

This was the height of the Cold War where some people claimed that "Reds were under the beds".

There was the great seven-week coal miners' strike in 1949 in Australia, allegedly caused by the communists. The strike affected power stations' ability to generate electricity. The gas supply was then also generated from coal. The steel industry had to suspend some operations and lay off workers. The Australian Labor Government bought in the Army to break up the strike.

There was also the "Petrov Affair" in 1954, when Soviet diplomat Vladimir Petrov defected from the Soviet embassy in Canberra and said there was a "nest of spies" in Australia masquerading as diplomats.

Liaison officers on the DP ships advised people fleeing communism not to join unions as they were seen as infiltrated by communists.

Following the Soviet invasion of Hungary in 1956, Australia received plane-loads of Hungarian refugees. There were images of them on the news, getting off the plane and crying. My father was a very strong man who never displayed emotion, but him seeing the refugees arrive from Hungary was the only time I ever saw him cry.

We would continually hear of individual horror stories of terror and escape. Hungarian Olympians sought asylum after the 1956 Olympics in Melbourne.

I remember we received a pamphlet in the mail on how to build an atomic bomb-proof shelter.

It was also the McCarthy era in the United States.

The "Cambridge Five" became news in Great Britain, as a group of upper-class Englishmen turned out to be Soviet spies.

The Australian Labor Party (ALP) split into two in 1955 because of alleged communist infiltration. The Democratic Labor Party (DLP) split from the ALP and was staunchly anti-communist. Allegedly, the ALP was infested with "commies". The DLP as a force in politics has now vanished.

There were those who thought that, since Latvia was now behind the "Iron Curtain", I must be a potential commie or a communist spy.

The Catholic Church was very vocal. They even had a prayer at the end of mass for the "conversion of Russia". One nun asked me if my parents had contacts overseas. I replied honestly, "yes". The stamps on the letters that arrived at our house from Latvia were Russian.

I didn't comprehend at the time what she was really asking, or why. In retrospect, she was probably asking if we had contacts with the Communist regime. Being very young and naïve, I didn't mention my parents were staunchly anti-communist.

At school, I met a boy whose father was a navigator in a Lancaster bomber who bombed Germany during World War II. My father was a bomber pilot on the "other side".

We shared aeroplane pictures and became good, lifelong friends. His father was a coal miner before the war, and after his time in the Air Force returned back to mining.

I went to an all-boys high school, Christian Brothers, in Wollongong. There was a mixture of different nationalities at high school, but the majority were still Anglo-Irish.

The teachers were nearly all "Brothers". There were very few secular teachers. The Brothers were very dedicated and said their main job was to make us men. In the last years at school, they would address us as "Mr" and use our surname.

I was placed in the "A" class, but when my Mum found out this class taught French and Latin she demanded I learn something that would be useful. I was then transferred into the "B" class which, among other subjects, taught technical drawing.

There was one school friend, Hans (now living in New Zealand), whom I still email, who said he was German. The borders changed after World War II and the region his parents came from is now part of Poland. His father was in the German Army and couldn't come out to Australia until three years after he and his mother came out.

When he started public school in Balgownie, he received similar treatment to what I'd received in Bowral. His mother moved him to a Catholic school and things improved. The exception was on weekends, when boys from the old school would catch him and beat him up.

There was another, now prominent, boy we called "Woatek". (He's now changed his name to a less Polish one.) His surname name indicated a typical Polish heritage, and he also had a hard time at school. He has been awarded an AM.

He said that one day, when his father was in a shoe shop, he spoke in a "foreign" language, and he was abused so badly he never spoke a language other than English again.

There was also one boy I remember, Henry, who had a distinctly Polish surname. His father changed the surname of the family to a typically Anglo-sounding name.

There was also a Peter, who recognised himself as of German heritage. He kept to himself, and when most boys joined the Australian Army Cadets he excluded himself. He was the odd one out.

After leaving school, we all followed different careers and drifted apart.

Many years later, in about 1991 when I was Construction Manager rebuilding Southern Copper, I had a young female graduate electrical engineer who was about to be retrenched as the project began winding down.

She asked me for a reference. She applied for a job and was accepted immediately by a Senior Manager from an electrical design company. She and her father thanked me profusely for the reference. The Senior Manager was Peter, who I hadn't seen since high school in 1964.

There may have been many more students in my time at school that suffered similar fates that I can't remember after 60 years. We didn't "compare notes".

The world after World War II in Germany was chaotic. A friend of ours had a Latvian father and a German mother. She was born in Nuremberg where her father was stationed and then drafted into the United States Army after the war.

I strongly doubt they would have conscripted a raw recruit with no military training to join the United States Army in a foreign land. I suspect he may have previously been in the German Army as a Latvian conscript during the hostilities. She sent me a copy of his United States Army enlistment papers.

In about year 3 in high school, a careers advisor came to the school and advised me that I should quit at the end of the year and get a trade apprenticeship. To leave school early was an opinion of an "expert", who made recommendations like this for a living. I believed him.

In retrospect, I think there may have been a bit of carryover from attitudes he had learnt as a boy in the late 1940s or early '50s. There also may have been an element of racism in his assessment.

He could also have been influenced by the policy of the Australian Government in the late '40s and early '50s. When they allowed DPs to come to Australia, all men regardless of previous qualifications or experience were classified as "labourers". The Immigration Department felt they didn't need people with skills – just labourers who wouldn't aspire to senior positions.

The skilled jobs and senior positions were for "Australians" and people from the Mother Country – Britain. They dismissed any documentation of European overseas qualifications as they considered they might have been forged.

The careers advisor said I would never be able to go to university. I told my father what he said and he disagreed. He said, "you're cleverer than that", and we argued. My Dad tried another approach. He promised that if I continued high school till the end he would buy me a car.

If the careers advisor hadn't told me I should quit school, I would have tried harder and not given up. Subsequently, I didn't try hard as it seemed pointless, but the lure of a car seemed a worthwhile goal. I continued going to high school and sat and passed the Leaving Certificate, albeit not very well.

The teaching techniques used then, from what I understand, were different from today's. There was one particular short, robust brother who saw I was struggling with trigonometry (i.e., sines, cosines, tangents, etc).

He said to me in the class, where everyone could hear, words to the effect of: "If you don't pass maths you will fail your Leaving". This clearly said to me what the facts were that I should be aware of.

At the end of the lesson told me quietly: "If you come to school on Saturday I'll help you with your maths". This gave me a way out.

My Dad bought me a 1942 Willies Jeep the year after I passed my Leaving Certificate. It was before 4WDs become popular. It was a heap of fun; I "rolled" it twice. Otherwise, it was junk as it was built with

1920s and '30s technology and was only designed to last 60 hours. It required constant maintenance.

I tried the same approach with my children. My daughter didn't accept the offer and left school early. She later went back to school, went to university and became a teacher.

My son accepted the car and finished high school.

Eventually, I proved to myself that the teachers in the public school in Bowral and the careers advisor in high school were wrong. I ended up at university, gaining a Masters of Engineering with honours. I also lectured in project management part-time at the University of Wollongong.

It didn't matter then to the teachers in Bowral Public School what they had allowed to happen where I first started.

My university study was all done on a part-time basis while I was working and raising a family.

Work

In 1964, I started working with Australian Iron & Steel, a subsidiary of BHP (the "Big Australian"). I began as a trainee for which I had to serve an apprenticeship to get the basic trade skills of engineering. The experience, exposure and training I received was the best I I've experienced or seen elsewhere in all the organisations I've worked for or with.

The Big Australian once incorporated Australian Iron & Steel (AI&S) and BHP Engineering. The thinking behind the basic training was: "If you can say with confidence you once did it yourself, no one will be able to pull the wool over your eyes and say something is impossible."

Wollongong University College (then a college of the University of NSW, now the University of Wollongong) was the concept of F M Mathews. He was the man responsible for the construction and development of the upgrade of AI&S in the 1950s.

I believe the type of training given by AI&S is no longer available and never again will be. This is mainly due to the reduction of employees from about 22,000 to about 3,000 and the reduction in heavy engineering and manufacturing in Australia. I believe the trainee intake when I started was about 200 trainees per year.

During my last years there I was in the Project Development Engineers Department. It consisted of Design, Procurement, Electrical, Civil, and Mechanical/Structural Steel Departments.

I was in the Mechanical/Structural Steel section, and the only one in the section with an Engineering certificate or degree. I had some very experienced and competent tradesmen to assist me with their particular areas of expertise.

I graduated through various supervisory roles then finally to an engineer on professional staff.

During upgrades of existing plants we would sometimes have shutdowns. It was very important to minimise downtime. I can remember at least twice working 13-hour night shifts continuously for a month, without a break.

These companies no longer exist. Blue Scope Steel, which replaced AI&S, is only a very small version of what it used to be.

In about 1979, after completing my Masters degree, I proposed computerising the current project management system from design, procurement and construction. Before that, everything required to build a project was done on a paper system. We also used the "fast track system". This is where erection started before the design was complete.

People didn't always have the latest or current information as things developed and changed. Things would be built to drawings that had to be amended later. Parts would be procured and built, but never used.

It was the fastest way, but to an "outsider" it may have seemed wastefully and chaotic. But by this method the plant being built was built faster and made productive earlier, to bring in revenue.

I had put almost all my efforts into the concept of computerisation of the system. Many obstacles were placed in my way. The concept was "shelved" because I couldn't say how many people could be replaced with this change.

In 2010 I worked for a company as Senior Project Manager, and the company had independently developed an identical system.

I became impatient, when BHP had just announced a $500 million expansion. I proposed that computerisation would improve the management of this work.

I noticed that very few people, if any, in higher positions in the steelworks had non-Anglo-sounding names.

I was promoted to head the new planning department for the expansion. We didn't have effective tools available at the time and had to rely on the mainframe computer and mountains of printouts, which people didn't read.

The joke was we produced the program and it was put on the shelf. It was replaced by the next month's program but never opened. It was too complex and voluminous but it was the best available.

There is a story that NASA developed two programs, the PERT and CPM programs, and placed the output on a wall. Someone decided it was top secret and arranged for a curtain to hide it. The curtain was never drawn until a man landed on the Moon.

I suggested a new electronic system based on standalone computers. This was also rejected as it was considered too expensive. Now, there are many project management tools on laptops.

I still believe we could have been world leaders in project management systems if I had been allowed to pursue my concepts.

BHP was a primary mining and steel production company. Project management, in spite of the enormity of the work we did – in the hundreds of millions of dollars – and the talent and expertise we had, was merely an overhead and not a revenue earner.

I had gained a great deal of valuable and diverse transportable experience in engineering construction and project management of large projects while I was with the "Big Australian". I was there for seventeen-and-a half years before I resigned.

When I met up with one of my colleagues about a year after I resigned, they said: "I hope you don't mind me saying this, but you're the biggest bastard I ever worked for, but it was enjoyable. You made us feel very important. It's not the same anymore."

My boss for about 10 years, a little more than a year later after I left, asked if he could leave BHP and come and work with us.

On another project several years later, my second-in-command asked me: "Why do you push so hard?" I replied: "Do you consider it wrong for me if I expect you to do your best?"

After I left BHP, two of my colleagues resigned from the BHP Construction Contracts Department and joined me in a business venture I had started.

On leaving, my manager at BHP, the Chief Development Engineer, wished me luck and quoted Brutus's passage from Shakespeare's *Julius Caesar*:

> There is a tide in the affairs of men,
>
> Which, taken at the flood, leads on to fortune;
>
> Omitted, all the voyage of their life
>
> Is bound in shallows and in miseries.
>
> On such a full sea are we now afloat;
>
> And we must take the current when it serves,
>
> Or lose our ventures.

After leaving BHP I worked with some small companies and some of Australia's largest project management and construction companies. It was in all the capital cities of Australia except Hobart and Darwin.

I also worked in many regional areas – Mt Isa, Kalgoorlie, Olympic Dam, the Bowen Basin, Mulwala, the Hunter Valley, Lismore, Wagga Wagga and Newcastle's Kooragang Island. I also worked for years in Papua New Guinea, Thailand and China and visited Korea, Japan and Germany as part of my work.

I've also worked with people of many different nationalities, which are too numerous to list. These projects are all complete stories in themselves and will be written about separately.

On my next birthday I will be 80 years old. I've gone back to university after more than 45 years. In that time, I've learnt a great deal about many different cultures and cultural practices.

My experiences in life, both with people and in engineering project work, have given me a very open mind. There's more than one way of thinking and behaving and achieving a result. This is a very different experience to that of a person who has had the same type of experience repeated many times, in the same organisation with the same types of people.

Landing in a different place, alone, not knowing the language and customs, unable to read the signs, being regarded as an oddity, can for some people be very challenging.

Above: Children in Sunday best at our first home in Bowral. From right: me (Vid), Brigita Oskerko, Janis Zozans, my brother Rudolfs, Doreen MacCallum, and another unknown friend.

Left: Mum and I. I'm in a pram by my Dad from scrap metal from a crashed aeroplane in the camp in Germany. Note the propeller at the back which would spin.

My father (far right) with some of his squadron when he was in the Latvian Air Force.

My father (far right) graduating from the Latvian Air Force.

Wanda and I just after our wedding ceremony in March 1968.

My Dad in a hot air balloon on his 80th Birthday, 1994.

My class at Bowral Public School, 1953. In those days, no one wore school uniforms. I am third row from the bottom, third from the right.

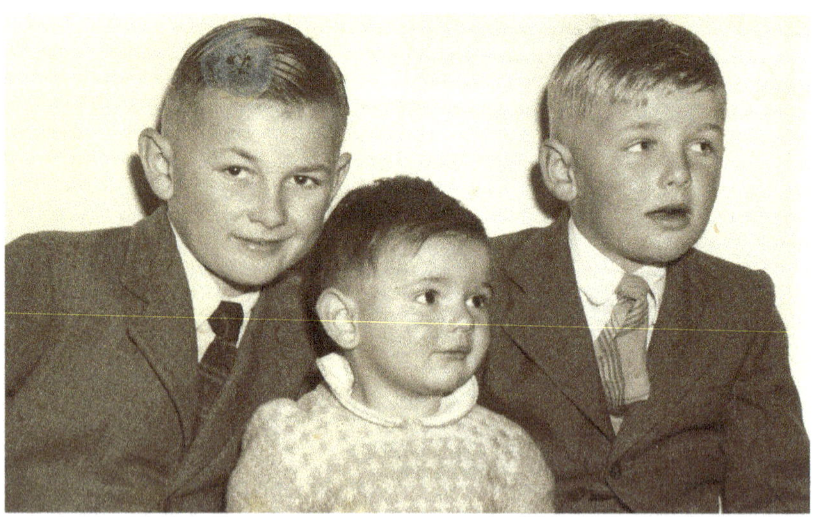

My brothers and I. From left, myself, Oskars and Rudolphs.

Wanda, my future bride, circa 1961.

Wanda and her family, circa 1964.

A postcard from Oldenburg-Ohmstede, Germany, where I lived with my family for a time. 'Lettische Kolonie' means Latvian Colony. It was originally a camp for Polish POWs and had been cleaned up when displaced persons, particularly women, arrived.

Above: Me (in fur hat) with relatives on the last day of my first trip to Latvia.

Top right: Me in front of an old hill fort that was besieged by the Teutonic Knights and all inhabitants killed.

Middle right: Me arriving at Riga Airport for the first time. From left: my niece Iveta, me, my son David and my step-brother Ojars.

Bottom right: Three generations – me, my son David and my father, and Oljars in the background..

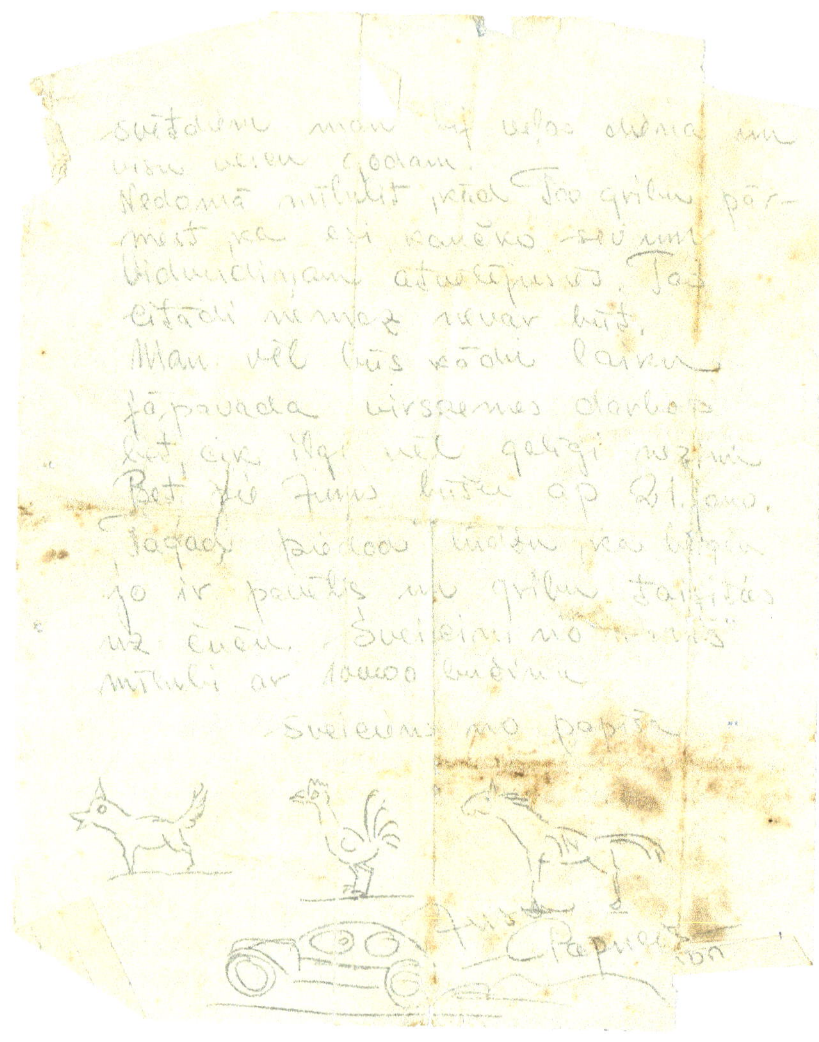

Letters from my father: My Dad was working in Sydney while my Mum and I were in the camp at Bathurst. He wrote many letters. This shows he included me by drawing pictures.

10.3.49.
Sydnejā.

Mani mīluši!

Ko Jums lai pasaku neko
jaunā nava. Tikai mana
sirds aizvo vennē pie Jums
un ir ar Jums, Milo mammiet
Par Jums domāju ļoti daudz
bet pagaidām nevaru neko
izdomāt. Ko todien no savan
turēts kabatos savin mīlulien
lai nosūtu ziemat nu par
lalu kas ir.
Milo Oldzīt man ļoti žēl, ka
nevaru Jums sagādat pātreiz
labākus dzīves apstakļus un
par to klusā vakara stundās
ļoti sāp sirds,
Paliekat nuli sveicināti ar
tukstots buču jam
Jūsu Papuets

Note date of the letter from Sydney – 10 Jan 1949. We arrived in Australia on 18 November 1948.

Me at Dobele Hill Fort which was the last stand before Namejs left.

Above: Copy of a Namejs ring given to most Latvian boys on their 18th Birthday.

Right: Al fresco lunch in Latvian summer. Blankets on chairs are not uncommon.

Top: Castle in Satzvey, near where my niece Rita lives in Germany.

Left: Me visiting the town in Bad Muenstereifel on my trip to visit Rita in Germany.

Me visiting the town in Bad Muenstereifel.

Nissen huts in at the Freilichtmuseum, in Kommern, Germany, similar to the ones we were accommodated in, in Bathurst. The huts in Bathurst are no longer there.

Me inside a Nissen hut. Notice the bed behind me and the hut's lack of internal lining. Where several families were in the same hut, the only separation was a curtain between them.

Imagined figure of a Curonian King in the 13th century.

Vidvuds

My parents named me Vidvuds Vidins.

This was a real problem when I started school as it wasn't a recognisable Anglo name and people had difficulty in pronouncing it, let alone remembering it.

The Latvians celebrate a "name day" as well as their birthdays. My name day falls on 11 June.

I was told that Vidvuds was an ancient Latvian hero's name. I liked to imagine that when I was born, Latvia was in deep turmoil after World War II and my father may have thought it needed a new hero.

Where we lived in Australia, in Bowral, there was a young girl named Doreen. She was the daughter of Mack, a Bowral dairy farmer, and his wife, who everyone called Mrs. Mack. I met Doreen when she was about five years old and have kept in touch with her all my life, even though we didn't see each other for years at a time.

Doreen was the first person who called me "Vid", and the name stuck. I went to her funeral in 2025.

It's remarkable how long simple acts of kindness are remembered, even after more than 70 years.

My mother didn't know the origin of my name when I first asked her as a teenager. There are few, if any, significant written records of life before the invasion of the Northern Crusaders in the 13th century. If there were any, they would have most likely been destroyed as being Pagan.

The only information I'm aware of was oral, passed down over generations. Written records started to be kept at about the end of the first millennium. This is when the Teutonic Knights invaded and written records were interpreted and recorded through their eyes. Ancient non-Christian beliefs weren't carefully documented.

After my Mum died, I found a small wooden box made by her youngest brother, Shasha, with some small mementos in it for me to keep.

Mum wrote that a very long time ago, people lived as hunter gatherers on the south side of the Baltic Sea. This region was where extinct Ancient Prussia was. The Ancient Prussians were not Germans as we know them – they were referred to as "Balts", i.e., people from around the Baltic Sea.

When knowledge of growing crops spread from Anatolia (the Asian part of Turkey) northwards, and as the weather got warmer, people prospered, multiplied and survived.

However, the amount of arable land became inadequate to feed everyone. People fought when they perceived boundaries were crossed. This developed into absolute chaos.

According to oral history, Vidvuds was a tribal chief, a "strong man" who established law and order. He realised that the root cause of the problems was that with the increased population there was inadequate available land. Due to the thawing of the ice caps and global warming, land became available further north, so he took those that wanted to follow him to what is now part of Latvia.

When I had my DNA tested, I found out there is a portion of the ancient Baltic Prussian in my genetics.

From reading published material, the now extinct Curonian language had elements of the now also extinct ancient Prussian language. There appears to be an apparent connection and some truth in what my mother wrote. It has been recorded that my father's ancestors with the surname Vidins have Curonian heritage.

From what I've read, this migration to what is now Latvia happened in the late Iron Age. Not much is written about this as it was before books were written in that part of the world.

There are some stones with runic inscriptions that have been found in Latvia, but these don't describe prehistory extensively. One can't write a great deal on stone.

Remaining written sources also note that before the invasion of the Teutonic Knights, the Curonians had what were called "Kings" that dominated the ancient Curonian portion of modern Latvia. They fished, made sea-worthy boats and raided and plundered Sweden before the advent of the Swedish Vikings.

My father once told me we were descended from Vikings. I didn't believe him at first, but I didn't forget it either. Vikings, I was taught at school, were from Norway, Sweden and Denmark. With research, I found it was true. Curonians were referred to as the "Eastern Vikings". They were originally fishermen, became good boat builders and sailors, then became pirates.

It is chronicled that the people from Sweden feared them. This was before what we know as the Scandinavian Vikings.

My father's name was *Arvids* mine is *Vidvuds*. I named my son David. If you know a little bit about the Italian language, which is my wife's heritage, "Da" means "of" or "from", as in Da Vinci, meaning "from Vichy". I like to think of my son's name as meaning "from Vid".

My mother's parents

My grandfather Janis (John) Dombrovskis fought the Germans in World War I in the Tsars Army. He also fought the Bolsheviks just after the war for Latvian independence. Latvia gained Independence in August 1920.

He was badly wounded in the last conflict and lost many fingers from one hand. The remaining fingers made his hand look very grotesque.

He was granted land as a result of his service in the War of Independence.

I knew him only as what I considered "a cranky old man". He was very resourceful – I saw him fashion a bent scythe handle from a green tree branch by exposing it to a fire and bending it to suit. He made his own beer from barley seed, which he spread on the floor to germinate.

He told me that during the Great Depression in the 1930s he would hunt deer in the forest with his army-issued firearm. To provide meat to feed his family, he always kept the firearm in his wagon.

He showed me how to cook "Jagerwurst", a German hunters sausage similar in texture to Italian salami. It was a dried, long, rectangular-shaped sausage that, when viewed from the end, was about 1 inch by ¾ inch.

You cut off about 6 inches then cut it longitudinally, but not all the way through, and pour vodka (at least proof + as below proof it wouldn't light) in the slot and light it. The burning vodka combined with the melting fat would cook and heat the meat. You could do this to avoid making a fire when hunting.

He also showed me how to cook fish (mainly pickled herring) in the bush, by wrapping them individually in wet newspaper and throwing them into the ashes of a small fire, along with unpeeled potatoes.

Sadly, my grandfather often reminisced about his friends – the young boys who were lost during the war.

He was granted land after Independence, built a home and worked the land. Then, in 1940, the Russians came. They confiscated his land to make it part of a Kolkhoz, a collective farm.

My grandfather had been a very proud soldier, and I have several photos of him in his army uniform, with highly polished black boots. He taught me how to polish mine "properly". He and my father told me you can tell a good man by three things:

- he has well-polished boots;
- he looks you straight in the eye; and
- he has a firm but not overpowering handshake.

Several years later, in the early 1960s, I was introduced to a Latvian girl by my mother. I wanted to impress her. I shook her hand much too hard, and she, I imagine, thought I was trying to bring her to her knees. Another lesson learnt.

My grandfather left Latvia, his home, before the end of the war. He would have been in his early 40s. I don't know if he went or was sent to Germany during the war.

His brother Antons Arnis, who, according to his daughter Ineta, didn't fight, changed his name from "Dombrovskis", which seems to have been "Latvianised" but with Polish or Lithuanian roots, to what he believed to be more a more Latvian name, "Mednis", which means "hunter". I don't know his first name, but there are several photos of my grandfather and his brother standing side by side, my grandfather in his uniform and his brother in a suit.

My grandfather had also left his brother and remaining friends behind. They were deported to Siberia. Alongside my grandmother Maria, he came to a strange foreign country, where they couldn't speak the language and had to start making a living again. They came to Australia later than my parents, on another boat, and were sent to a new DP camp in Bonegilla, not in Bathurst as we were.

Having been a soldier and a farmer in Latvia, and now without land, when he came to Australia he could only obtain menial work. He could, however, speak Polish, Latvian, German, Russian and Lithuanian fluently.

Because he learnt English later in life, his English was poor.

In Australia he always had a rifle in his house.

He got very upset with me when my Mum told him I had wagged school because I was being beaten up and was afraid of going to school. I received a belting from him.

His pride and joy in Australia was his first motorcycle with a sidecar. He called it his "pletska".

After retirement he did a lot of volunteer work for the church.

When he got older he began to drink a lot more. This was as a result of what is now called PTSD. It wasn't recognised as a problem or treatable while he was alive.

When he was drunk, he lamented the boys that died in the war for what eventually happened. The end result was practically nothing.

There was also a Peter Dombrovskis who came to Australia as a DP. He settled in Tasmania and was a renowned wilderness photographer. Unfortunately, he drowned in 1996 in a canoe accident. He provided many photographs used in the infamous Gordon-below-Franklin River protests. Most Latvians, except a very few, weren't allowed to have a surname until after the Napoleonic wars. I don't know what, if any, his connection with my grandfather was but I guess it's highly likely there is one.

My grandmother Maria, born in 1896, was also a remarkable lady. She was also multilingual and well educated for the time. During World War I, when she was a young girl, she was sent from Latvia by the Tsarist Russians to work in the Post Office.

She was transported from Latvia, which was the very west of the Russian Empire to the very far east of the Russian Empire to Manchuria. Manchuria was the eastern part of China before the concession made to Russia during the Opium Wars in the mid-1800s.

On my trip to Latvia in 1991, it took me about 10 hours to fly over Siberia. I can't even imagine or guess how long it must have taken on a World War I vintage steam train.

After the Russian surrender to the Germans in 1917 it became absolute chaos in Russia as the Bolshevik Revolution took over. My grandmother had to get back home. I can't imagine how long it took her, but it must have taken a lot longer with the chaos.

She told me that when she was going back home she left her suitcase outside a train station toilet. It was stolen, with all her possessions and paperwork.

She managed to get back to her own home town.

She had grown up a bit since leaving, and looked different. She asked where her father was. She mentioned his name but nobody had heard of him. Everyone was suspicious of people they didn't immediately recognise, due to the confusion of the War of Liberation, the people fleeing from danger and spies everywhere.

The Latvians had the help of the German "Iron Division", the German "Fried Corps", the Baltic Germans, and the White Russians ("Mensheviks") to help fight the Bolsheviks. But the Germans turned on the Latvians when they realised the Latvians wanted independence.

Many Latvian Commanders died from "friendly fire" from the Germans.

My grandmother then mentioned her father's nickname (I believe it was something like "Soromouse") and they immediately recognised the name and my grandmother.

Latvia was a real mess and in chaos after World War I. The "Baltic Germans" were fearful that the Bolsheviks would confiscate their land, but also feared the Latvians – that if they won they would also have designs on their land.

Some Latvians, like the "Latvian Red Rifles" supported the Bolsheviks. Lenin chose the Latvian Red Rifles as his personal bodyguards, as he felt they were the only ones he could really trust.

The British Navy was also involved and shelled "enemy" positions and lost some British soldiers in Latvia. These British soldiers are now buried in Jelgava, Latvia. I was very surprised to see them buried there as I read they only supplied sea support.

The Polish Army assisted the Latvians to fight the Bolsheviks in the south of Latvia, and the Estonians helped fight the Germans in northern Latvia.

There was no such thing as a front line. There were many fronts that moved and changed quickly.

Eventually everyone was ready for independence, and they signed a peace treaty with the Bolshevik government in Russia in August 1920. Many Baltic Germans had their lands confiscated, but some stayed until just before the Soviet invasion. It was not a good start for the country.

My grandmother and grandfather bought the property in town on Walker Street where we first lived in Bowral. My Dad, Mum, brother and I then moved to Daphne Street in Bowral. My youngster brother Oskars was born in Bowral.

My grandmother purchased a pregnant cow and chickens and maintained a large veggie garden in Bowral. When my wife and I visited her she always had veggies to give us from her extensive garden to take home.

She'd make all her own butter and cheese. She made her own sauerkraut and pickled her cucumbers in a large (about 200-litre) wooden barrel under the house. I would occasionally go under the house when I was young and pick out a cucumber before it was completely pickled. I thought it tasted much better than when it was fully fermented.

I made my own sauerkraut and pickled cucumbers many years later when I had a farm in Robertson. The result was almost as good as I remember it.

I remember the two of us kneeling on the grass behind the house, picking a wild broadleaf weed which my grandmother called something like "scarbenes". With these leaves she would make a soup. It was sour and very bitter. I didn't like it, but sometimes in the evening it was the main and only meal.

I remember her hatching chickens in a shoe box lined and covered with a rag, then placing it on the edge of the slow-combustion stove for warmth. She checked it often and it worked well

My grandfather would shoot the calf from the cow when it got older and dress it in the backyard. He would go out with a scythe he had made and cut hay to store for the cow over winter.

My grandfather died in 1971, before my grandmother, from pneumonia. After he died, my grandmother was seduced into one of those communal, American-style charismatic religions and gave her land and house to the "church". She said she eventually realised what was going on and, with her youngest son Shasha, escaped from the "church".

Her one-acre block in Bowral would have been worth a lot of money then, but now she was penniless. She came to live with my mother and father before ending up in a retirement home. She was 96 when she passed in 1992 and is buried next to my grandfather in Bowral Cemetery.

My mother's sister Helena was married in Germany to a Latvian named Peters. He was the accordion player in the family.

I had a large copy of the Frederick McCubbin painting 'The Pioneers' on the wall at my farm. One day, my uncle stood looking at it for a particularly long time. I asked him what he was seeing. He replied that his father was not a Latvian Independence veteran so he wasn't granted cultivated land after the war. However, if he went into the forest he could clear a patch and it would be his.

He said he would tie his horse with a long rope to the top of the tree and dig and cut around the roots on one side and the tree would be pulled over by the horse. He'd cut the wood to make a log cabin. He then acquired a large, flat-bottom bucket which he would tie to his horse and they would excavate the dams. They would plant oats in the excavation then harvest them. Then he would allow water to fill the dams and grow carp for the market. This would sustain the family. He abandoned the farm when he fled during World War II.

When he visited Latvia in the 1990s he went to his father's farm. The home was gone. The place was overgrown and the dams were broken and empty. This really hurt him. It was as if his forebears had never existed.

Now, when I see the McCubbin painting it triggers this memory of him. Now it means more to me than just a good early Australian painting.

My uncle had a .22 calibre rifle and a shotgun as long as I knew him. When the first gun amnesty came he gave me his pump action shotgun. I had a farm and was allowed to have one. He preferred to give it to me than surrender it for money.

This may have been a result of his experience of having to surrender his arms at the end of World War II. After surrendering, he had the feeling of being completely vulnerable in the hands of his captives. The soldiers, when they surrendered, were put into a hastily constructed prison camp in an open field.

Prison camp conditions, where people that were interned had been in the German Army after World War II, have been recorded as being hastily built, inadequate and atrocious. They were overcrowded and without shelter. Transport routes in Germany had been destroyed or damaged. Logistics was planned firstly for the front line troops, not POWs.

Buildings had been bombed or shelled. There was also a huge number (approximately 10 million) of non-military DPs in Germany who had to be catered for. The housing of German POWs was below the bottom of this list.

There was no shelter available. POWs dug pits to sleep in and there was a lack of food and medical help. A great many of them died.

To ease the congestion in the POW camps, the captors separated the German National soldiers and those that the Germans had "conscripted" after 1943 from lands they had conquered. These "conscripts" were allowed day-release from the prison camp.

My uncle said he was bored as there was nothing to do, so he would go to local farms to find some work. He'd work a whole day for a widow and she would give him a potato for his efforts.

My father's father

I never met my grandfather on my father's side. I believe he died in Latvia in the early 1950s. Regrettably, I never knew his name or when he was born.

He was one of those descended from the "Curonian Kings" who retained a degree of independence after the invasions by the Northern Crusaders. One of the several concessions made for the kings, after the hostilities ceased, were that his ancestors were allowed to retain their surname and other benefits. They were allowed to keep their land.

The privileges they were initially allowed were slowly "whittled" away over the many invasions over the centuries by other countries such as Sweden, Denmark and Russia. I understand that before World War I he was an estate manager over the area for possibly one of the Baltic Germans.

My father was born in the Manor House in 1914.

After the War of Independence, those who were descended from the "Curonian Kings" who had any special privileges that remained over many centuries now had them withdrawn. The estate was subdivided and parcels of land were redistributed to the War of Independence veterans.

I believe my grandfather moved to the city of Jelgava. My father mentioned that he was standing outside one evening, at the end of World War I, watching the sky light up, and his father said they were burning down Jelgava Palace.

Jelgava Palace is the largest Baroque-style palace in the Baltic. It was restored after World War I, destroyed again during World War II and restored again after. It is now used as the University for Agriculture.

I never heard much from my father about his mother except that she ushered him into the house after he was staring at a red aeroplane fly over.

My brothers

I had two younger brothers, Rudolfs, who has a son Ruben, and Oskars, who had three sons. Rudolfs is still alive today, while Oskars passed away some years ago.

Rudy was born in Bathurst DP camp. He lived in Western Australia for about 40 years, in Boulder in the Goldfields with his son Ruben on one of the many mine sites in Western Australia.

He married a divorced woman who claimed to have German heritage. She already had several children from a previous marriage. She was a Seventh Day Adventist and had strong fundamentalist views. I believe she was accepted, but Rudy didn't, as far as I know, follow her beliefs.

Oskars died in his 30s from cancer, when his boys were still young. His sons married and had children and are now scattered around Queensland and the Northern Territory.

Wanda, my wife, and my children

Wanda's father, Giuseppe (Joe) Forner, was born in a small ancient village called Aslo in the Veneto region of Northern Italy. The village goes back to pre-Roman times. Joe's surname is not originally from that region. The surname "Forner" originates from either France or Austria. Northern Italy was invaded and occupied many times by both countries.

Joe was born in 1921, just one year after Mussolini took power. The house where he was born was over 600 years old.

We have a large picture of Aslo in our home, which he gave me and which I treasure. He also kept several books about the village. Aslo features the remnants of an old Roman fort. Joe told me that as a child he threw stones at the walls. They also had an opera house in town. This was dismantled and taken to the United States after World War II.

Joe was drafted into the Italian Army for World War II. He didn't say much about it and never mentioned that he saw any action.

Italy surrendered in September 1943. The Germans marched in and gave the Italians two options: go into a POW camp or go to the Russian front. He chose to be a POW. The other option was to join one of the many partisan groups.

Italy was a complete mess after the surrender as there were no jobs. Homes and infrastructure had been bombed and/or destroyed and there was little shelter or food.

My parents and I were taken by train to Genoa, Italy to catch a converted Liberty ship, the Castel Bianco, to Australia.

My mother told me she had never seen poverty in Italy like that, not even in Germany. They gave some of their rations to the destitute children who were begging on the streets.

Almost anyone in Italy who was in the public sector up until the surrender had been a member of the Fascist Party. Up to 15,000 fascists were purged or killed up until 1946 by the partisans. There was a complete social and administrative collapse. There was absolutely no work for Joe in Italy after the war.

After being released from a POW camp, Joe went to work in Switzerland. He would come "home to Italy" only occasionally.

Joe didn't want to talk much about what happened, but when I offered on several occasions to pay for his ticket to see his brother in Italy, he declined.

Wanda has been back to Italy several times. According to Wanda, her uncle proudly showed her a medal he received for being a Partisan.

When Joe and his family immigrated to Australia in May 1955 he was sent with his wife Angelina and my future wife, Wanda, to the cane fields in Queensland to cut cane. Wanda was born in Italy in 1950.

Cutting cane was once considered as "Kanaka's" work, where people from the Pacific Islands were "blackbirded" to Australia to establish and work in the sugar cane industry. Most were deported later after Australia's Federation and the implementation of the White Australia policy.

They couldn't find sufficient what they considered as real "white men" to do the work. After World War I, many Italians had immigrated to Australia to escape Mussolini. Many had gone to the cane fields in Queensland.

The conditions were very primitive, and Joe and his family were originally housed in corrugated iron sheds. Angelina was isolated and home alone with small baby Wanda in a strange country, while Joe cut cane.

Angelina mentioned one particular incident to me several times. An "Aussie" came around to where she lived with a bunch of bananas. He gave her some. When she'd had enough she said, "basta, basta". The man didn't understand and considered she was ungrateful and swearing at him. In Italian, "basta" means 'enough'.

At the time, Italians were considered "not quite white enough" but they had a strong work ethic. Some bought farms and formed collectives. There was a great deal of prejudice towards the Italians when they first came to Australia in the 1920s, and later after World War II.

They were considered cowards when thousands surrendered en masse in North Africa during World War II. They obviously didn't want to support Mussolini's dream but also didn't want to appear anti-fascist with the inherent consequences.

There was also resentment in Australia when captured Italian POWs were bought to Australia. They weren't considered a threat and were allowed to go on day-release. This was to assist with agricultural work on farms when the "real white Australians" were fighting.

They were referred to by Australians as "dirty dagos", "wogs", "spags" and "eyeties". Many had migrated to Australia after Mussolini took power, and went to the Goldfields in Western Australia. They were preferred by the managers as they could be easily exploited and often worked very hard for less than normal pay.

There were major riots in Kalgoorlie and Boulder in 1934 where a hotel and several Italian premises were burnt down.

Italians also ate different foods and had different eating habits to the "locals". They cooked food "swimming in oil" and didn't use the customary fat or dripping. They ate fish bait before it was later rebadged as calamari, now a sought-after seafood. They ate sardines and offal.

The Italian POWs who transferred to Australia developed an inexpensive recipe to supplement their POW rations. This was unique to Australia and called "coniglio con spaghetti".

Rabbits were plentiful. They ran wild and bred prolifically. They were in plague proportions, and free. All one had to do was catch one, which was very easy in those days.

There was also plenty of wheat in Australia. Wheat=flour=spaghetti. There was also a red wine made by these prisoners to match. They gave it an Australian name: "Rabbit and Spaghetti".

When Joe died he was cremated. Wanda's mother, Angelina, died later. She asked that her husband's urn with his ashes be interred with her, with him in her arms.

The standard fare here in Australia before that was "meat and three veg." Sausages were either devon, eaten cold, or saveloy's cooked by various means. Ham was also available as well as corned beef in a tin. The "new Australians" that arrived were used to a greater variety of sausages.

The irony is that now the "Mediterranean diet" is considered the healthiest in Australia's climate. And people now brag about their "spag bol" recipes.

Beer and tea were the standard beverages. These newcomers drank "plonk" and coffee. The "plonk" drunk by "locals" was initially a sherry or port concealed in a brown paper bag to disguise what it actually was.

Wine became respectable with advent of the German-style sweet white wines in the early 1960s. They started with various versions of Rhine Rieslings, then the flagon, then this developed into a Coolabah cask, often referred to as "Chateau Cardboard". Australia now has some wines that rate among the best in the world. I've purchased and drunk Australian wines in China, Riga in Latvia, and Germany.

Wanda's DNA shows she has French, Austrian and Italian genetics as a result of the many invasions of Northern Italy. To our surprise, she also has some Baltic genes.

My Mum wanted me to marry a Latvian girl. She introduced me to a few but there was no "magic" there. They also made me feel a bit uncomfortable.

Wanda was a very beautiful girl and won "Miss Berkeley High" at school. The attraction was surprising as Latvians and Italians are almost diametrically opposite in personality. Latvians generally are said to be aloof and tend to stand back. They normally don't say much. Italians generally behave in the almost opposite manner.

Wanda and I are very different. People that have met me and then meet Wanda say: "She's really a nice person." I guess that says it all.

What I don't have, she has. She is my perfect better half. Wanda and I may not agree on everything but there's a respect for the other's views. Mum eventually warmed to her and wholeheartedly accepted her.

As of time of publication, we have been married for 58 years.

We don't speak each other's languages. We have two children, Tania and David, five grandchildren and two great-granddaughters.

We named Tania after "Tania Verstak" who was also a European immigrant to Australia. She won Miss Australia and also won Miss International. My grandmother was a bit upset as "Tania" was a Russian Name. Mum told her, it doesn't matter here.

Russia, December 1991

Latvia had become an independent country again just after the Baltic "Singing Revolution" in 1989. This was when about 2 million people across Estonia, Latvia and Lithuania, from Tallinn, Riga to Vilnius, joined hands and sang for their independence and freedom.

Latvia held a referendum for independence in March 1991 to free it from the Soviet Empire. The vote was overwhelmingly in favour (74.9%) of independence which was restored on 21 August 1991.

My father, who was just over 77 years old at the time, had not seen his brother and two sisters since about 1943 – about 48 years ago.

However, the Russians were still in control until the official handover, and the removal of the Russian troops was to be by 31 August 1994. My parents now felt relatively safe to go back to Latvia.

I arranged to take them to Latvia to see their siblings again. My father's brother and sisters had been taken to Siberia and had survived. My father also had a son to his first wife. He had first met his son a few years before when I had arranged to bring him to Australia for a holiday.

It had been nearly half a century since he had seen his son, and never met his son's wife or his granddaughter and grandson.

The only way we could arrange the trip back to Latvia for my parents was during my Christmas break from work. We had to travel separately because of timetables and my limited leave from work. We were on different flights – my father, mother and son flew on one plane and I flew on another.

I obtained a Russian visa for myself. My parents and son had separate visas. I flew from Sydney to Tokyo with Qantas, then from Tokyo to Moscow with Aeroflot.

Aeroflot was a bit of an experience. The plane flew over Siberia at night and it was very dark as it was almost mid-winter. Occasionally, I could see a single light on the ground. I then realised how vast Siberia was. The flight took 10 hours, with snow on the ground all the way and an occasional single light.

The flight stewardesses were more like female sumo wrestlers than the petite ones I was used to. They served dinner during the flight – a piece of boiled, very fatty belly pork and two pieces of what I later realised was bread. The bread was black and hard like a stale bread bun. I couldn't digest it so asked for something I expected they would have. Russians, I believed, always had vodka.

The hostess said it cost US$8. I was shocked. It was more than one pays for a small sample bottle on a plane in Australia.

I was hungry and found it hard to eat the fatty pork and the rock-hard bread. I agreed to the vodka. The hostess brought me a bottle. I said it was too much, and she replied: "Only half a litre … not too much".

There were many very pretty young women on board. They had goods stored in the aisle, making it practically impossible to go to the toilet. I suspected they might be "ladies of the night" and were bringing home goods purchased with the money they'd earnt.

An older woman from the group came and sat next to me and started speaking in broken English. She told me the girls were ballet dancers who had spent a month in Singapore ballet dancing and dancing traditional folk dances. They had bought presents home as gifts for Christmas.

I landed in Moscow and went through immigration. The customs officer sat in a small booth and looked at me suspiciously. When he stared, I shuddered. He looked positively evil, as if he was peering into my very soul and looking to see if I would flinch.

I mentioned this experience to my son. He said that he and my parents had the same experience. My father was completely "rattled" as he was trying to explain the purpose of his visit to this official in broken Russian.

After this, I went to wait at the baggage carousel. The airport was dark, dirty and dingy.

An announcement was made, and when it was half finished I realised it was in English pronounced with a heavy Russian accent.

I picked up my bag and I didn't know what to do next. A well-dressed girl with a brightly coloured Russian scarf approached me and asked if I was a tourist. She forced a smile. I said I was, and she took me to a waiting taxi.

The taxi driver tried to open the boot of the taxi but the key wouldn't turn. It was frozen. He put his hand over the lock and waited what seemed a few minutes then tried the key again, and it worked.

On the way to the hotel, the windscreen often froze and the driver had to use the wipers, which only seemed to be half effective as the windscreen kept icing up.

I looked at the snow on the ground, the bare, stark, leafless trees that looked black against the white snow, and thought to myself, I now know why some sombre Russian music sounds like it does. It was the Russian equivalent of the didgeridoo in Australia's outback.

We drove to the Belgrade Hotel. The lobby was dark and dingy. The ceiling lights were dusty and I could see they were covered with dirty fingerprints. A girl behind the counter said, "passport", in a manly voice. I gave her my passport and waited for what seemed like many minutes. I got nervous and caught her eye. She responded: "Next".

I went to the next counter and gave a girl my Visa card and waited. When I caught her eye, she said: "Next". I waited, and another girl handed me back my passport and Visa card. I waited again, and the next girl behind the counter said: "Next".

I went and got my key and waited. I watched others, and went to another girl who gave me the room number. I had to ask where the stairs were. I was pointed to a door.

It took seven people to book me in and point me to the lift.

I had paid what I would pay for a four-star hotel in Australia and what I got looked like a cheap one-star hotel room. There was a shower, a single bed or cot, a doona, a pillow and a TV. That was all.

My initial instincts were to leave immediately … but where would I go? I didn't speak Russian, nor did I know where else to go. It was also snowing outside, and I had paid for the room.

I unpacked and watched Russian TV where the good guys were depicted as Russian selfless heroes and the bad guys were English-speaking or at least had American accents.

In Australia, we're deluged with American films, where the Americans are always the "good guys" and the only people who can save everyone.

The next day, the hotel arranged for me a female guide who took me to Red Square. The first thing I noticed were the many old, muzzle-loading cannon barrels that were lying on the raised podium of a building. I imagined they were cannons left behind by Napoleon during his retreat from Russia.

Guards with guns seemed to be everywhere.

After the official tour I had some time left before my flight to Riga, so I walked the streets sightseeing. The streets were practically empty, like on a Sunday in Australia in the 1950s.

I was wearing a leather bomber jacket and a sheepskin hat. I was obviously a foreigner. I was approached by a young man who offered me a genuine Siberian fox hat, which I bought. He also offered me caviar he had in his pocket which I declined. He then ran away, saying in broken English that the police were watching us.

I found the Pushkin Museum. I was stunned at the number of French Impressionist paintings. There was also a copy of Michael Angelo's *David* which stood in the foyer. It was awe-inspiring and spectacular. I guessed it would have been about 12-feet high.

That evening, I went to the hotel restaurant. I looked at the menu, wanting something typically Russian. The waiter told me that each of the choices I'd selected was unavailable. I settled for sturgeon and a bottle of Georgian white wine.

I was the only guest in the restaurant. The male waiter was very attentive. The bill was 45 rubles. He gave me the bill and I took out my Visa card. He had apparently never seen a Visa card before. He directed me to reception and took my winter coat as security.

I withdrew US$50 and asked for the amount in rubles. They gave me what was virtually a shoe box full of paper rubles. I stuffed them into my pockets and under my shirt and went back to the restaurant.

I thought the bill couldn't be correct, as converted into Australian dollars it was only 45 cents, which included a bottle of wine.

I pulled out 45 Rubbles and looked at the waiter. He was astonished at the amount of money I had under my shirt.

I used the currency conversion my step-brother had told me when he visited Australia. The currency conversion on my trip started off as 90 rubles per Australian dollar. This equates to the meal with a bottle of wine costing me less than 50 cents.

I gave the waiter a 20-ruble tip (about 20 cents). By his reaction I thought he was about to hug me.

I also went to a Russian "supermarket" while in Moscow. The market was very spartan by Australian standards. I saw a large Babushka doll which I considered essentially Russian but pre-Soviet. The Babushka dolls were invented before the Russian Revolution.

I went to the pretty girl behind the counter, who had a sombre look on her face, and she gave me a piece of ripped paper with a price on it. Then I had to go to the next girl to pay. I didn't have enough money. The price was about 1,700 rubles, which was a whole stack of notes – the equivalent of A$17. I counted what I had with me and realised I didn't have enough.

I indicated to the cashier to hold the doll for me as it appeared to be the last one on the shelf.

I went back to my hotel, withdrew 2,000 rubles and went back to the market. I was happy the cashier understood what I had gestured. After paying for the doll, I offered her the remaining 300 rubles. She immediately handed it back. I offered it to her again. A whole crowd then gathered around us, staring.

The girl seemed to be embarrassed, so I said thank you – "pashalts" – and left. To me, it was only a small tip.

Thinking about it later, it must have been unusual to give tips in Russia, especially so much money – 300 rubles was only about $3 to me which is what we would call loose change in Australia. She may have thought I was paying for her "services" that night.

I contrasted Moscow, which was considered a "Second World country", with Bangkok in Thailand. I had worked in Bangkok earlier that year. Thailand was considered a "Third World country" – it was like comparing "chalk and cheese".

In Bangkok, the city would come to life and glow at night. There was plenty of noise, coloured lights at night, and street vendors everywhere with carts selling consumer goods. There were restaurants everywhere and people haggling over the prices, and the sidewalks were full of pleasant, happy people smiling all the time.

The streets would be congested with cars, scooters, motorbikes and other vehicles. It could take up to three hours to get from one side of the city to the other because of the traffic.

Moscow was about as opposite to that as one could imagine. The streets were almost devoid of vehicles and people. I remember seeing a few old Russian re-engineered versions of the American 1940s Packard. They would have originally been used by the communist elite.

If I graded Moscow I would have classified it as a poor Fourth World.

I was amazed that abacuses were used in Moscow shops for adding up. In Thailand, nearly all vendors had an electronic calculator which they would use to calculate then price then turn around to show you.

No one in Russia that I could see had an electronic calculator or even an adding machine. I bought an abacus as a keepsake. I still have it but can't use it properly.

On the way home at Moscow Airport sometime later, I had time to spare and needed a haircut. There was an old Babushka wearing a dress. It looked similar to a dress an old woman would wear around the house. She was also wearing a head scarf. She ran a hairdresser in the airport. She cut my hair and fussed and fussed. She then got some hot irons in my hair to give it a curl. She happily chatted in Russian and I didn't understand a word.

The haircut cost 50 rubles (about 50 cents). I gave her 100 rubles, and grasped her hand and closed it when she tried to give me the change. She grabbed me and danced, swirling me around, and smothered my cheeks with kisses.

During my short stay in Russia, over a few weeks the exchange rate went from 90 to 120 rubles a dollar.

I went to the toilet at the airport. It smelt badly of urine. There were two old Babushkas sitting on a bench outside the door. When I was leaving, one chased me. I quickened my pace and she gave up.

In another toilet I had a similar experience and guessed they were responsible for cleaning the urinals and sat outside expecting to get paid.

I flew to Riga the next day. Riga was still dominated by the Russian system and Russians when we arrived.

My father, mother and son were waiting for me with my step-brother, Ojars, and his daughter, Iveta. She had a bunch of flowers, albeit a bit wilted, but it was the middle of winter.

We got into the car and were approached by some tall Russian soldiers, who indicated, by tapping on the window with the barrel of a machine pistol, for us to wind down the window so they could see our papers. It was a bit unsettling but Ojars and Iveta didn't seem to be perturbed. Apparently, this was considered normal to them.

After a few days, my son would fly to Switzerland to meet some friends we'd met in Papua New Guinea. I took him to the international airport in Moscow. We sat down at a restaurant for a meal and the waitresses kept chatting and didn't come over to us. I raised my arm to catch their attention. I went through a few items on the menu, which was written in both English and Russian. To my surprise, all the food on the menu was unavailable.

I took my son to what we may call a "Russian fast food outlet" or cafeteria at the airport. I chose a few items that looked a bit unusual but I imagined were edible. My son wouldn't eat any of them.

He flew to Switzerland, met Ziggy and Francisca and spent some time skiing. From Switzerland he flew to Holland to meet a woman who was an old friend of mine from Australia who had moved to Holland.

He then flew to Italy to stay with Wanda's relatives. He was alone and had only a very basic, schoolboy's grasp of Italian. He was by himself and was upset with his Mum who had made all the arrangements.

Some police rescued him and took him to where he wanted to go. He later remarked that he was terrified with their driving through the narrow streets and the guns they had in the police car.

I had admired a samovar that was on the shelf in my step-brother's home. It belonged to his mother. Ojars gave it to me. It was a typical classical pre-communist Russian teapot. It was silver, about 18 inches high, bulbous and included a tap. Hot water and tea are added in the top and it has a small drawer underneath where a fire is lit to keep the tea warm. It's basically a large, old-fashioned, self-contained teapot.

My parents had to get back to Moscow to fly home. They had prepaid plane tickets but their travel plans changed and they had to catch a train from Riga to Moscow. Apparently there wasn't enough fuel at the time for the plane to fly from Riga to Moscow.

On the way home I checked in at Moscow Airport, and when I picked up my luggage I noticed the lock had been broken. My clothes, the Babushka doll and the samovar given to me by my step-brother were all there but some other smaller items were missing. This shocked me. I reasoned that if someone could break into my bag to steal something they could also put something in.

After that I always had a very solid, lockable bag made of hard, heavy plastic that couldn't be opened and couldn't be put in the cargo hold for travelling.

In all my experiences in Russia, I only saw one person smile. It was the girl who met me at Moscow Airport and took me to the taxi. The smile seemed to me not really genuine but fabricated.

Riga

My father's home town was the city of Jelgava. On our trip, when he had time, he walked around town to see what he could recognise, but everything had changed or was "Russified".

He found the street where he had lived. He remembered it had been called "Vidvuds Street" but he said the name was changed to "Vladimir Street".

My half-brother's daughter, Iveta, could speak reasonably good English. My Latvian was practically non-existent. It was my first language and I once could speak it fluently. I hadn't spoken it for 40 years – I could understand an occasional word but could no longer speak it.

Latvian is unusual as it's one of the closest languages to the ancient Indo-European languages, with very little if any Latin or Greek language influence.

Iveta acted as a tour guide to show me the sites in Riga, which was a relatively short train trip away from Jelgava.

I was scolded by Iveta when I wanted to negotiate for an amber necklace, as I always did in Thailand. She said many things I couldn't or didn't grasp or put into context at the time.

One story she told me was how the Latvians had torn up the cobbled streets in Riga, made barricades, and waved their once-banned flag, protesting for independence. They sung banned songs, expecting the Russian tanks accompanied by troops to attack.

She said that restaurants in the area fed the protestors behind the barricades for free during the protest. I didn't appreciate it at the time, but I later realised that she was one of the protestors. I asked myself, would I have had the courage to do that? I don't have an answer.

We went to an ice cream shop and she bought me ice cream. I questioned eating ice cream in the middle of winter. She responded: "We don't have sufficient electricity to make ice cream in summer."

While we were sitting there chatting in English, a stranger came and sat at our table. I considered this the height of rudeness as there were plenty of other free tables. I was going to say something, but Iveta touched my hand and I didn't say anything. Iveta didn't think this was unusual. I suspect the stranger may have been KGB – I don't know.

Iveta must have seen I was a little bit tired of walking and asked me if I had an American dollar. I replied "Yes". She then asked me to wait there and she fetched a taxi. I think the taxi trip was a dollar or two.

We went to the Dome Cathedral, which had a massive organ, and listened to a recital. I found the cathedral unusual as, after damage during many wars, parts of it had been replaced by the latest architectural styles. The oldest, undamaged part was Romanesque. The next-oldest part was early Gothic, with narrow, high windows. The next part was late Gothic, with wide windows, and the newest rebuilt part was Baroque. I could almost count the number of wars in the city by the number of different architectural styles used in the repairs.

We went to the Parliament. There were armed guards there, and I said I was a bit surprised. Iveta said there were Russian rogues around who wanted things to remain as they were.

She directed me to a film made by a journalist who was reporting during the transition. He was shot by the Russians but was still reporting. His words were recorded with each shot. He died reporting.

There were still defensive ancient walls in parts of the city. After the reoccupation in 1944, the population of Latvia was depleted by about 30%. This was due to war casualties, deportation to Siberia and escape to the West.

The Russians repopulated the city with people from Russia and its provinces. There was a deliberate policy to make the country more Russian.

Teaching the Latvian language was either forbidden or strongly discouraged as it was considered by the Russians to be a dead language.

All potential "enemies of the people" were sent to Siberia. This happened to my uncle and two of my aunts. They survived. As mentioned earlier, a cousin of mine, a Captain Vidins, was "taken to the forest".

My uncle mentioned that as they were being deported they would write notes or letters on paper to their loved ones and throw them out of the rail cars, hoping someone would pick them up and post them home.

The Russians would fill the void thus created by the importation of Ethnic Russians from other parts of Russia. This was their modus operandi:

- They would offer them subsidised housing.
- They collectivised the land.
- They suppressed the Latvian language and customs.
- All teaching in school had to be in Russian and in Cyrillic script.
- All documentation had to be in Russian and in Cyrillic script.
- They burnt or destroyed all books that didn't agree with the communist ideal.
- They schooled the children in the benefits of communism.

- They forbade Latvians from singing certain songs or displaying the ancient Latvian flag. (The Latvian flag is one of the oldest in the world.)
- When jobs became available, they would be filled first with Russian émigrés regardless of their qualifications.
- If there was an insufficient number of Russian émigrés, they filled these vacancies with fluent Russian speakers.
- Finally, if there weren't enough Russian speakers they would fill the positions with qualified Latvian citizens.

There was retribution for anyone whom they suspected could be disloyal or challenge the system. People who received letters from the West were under suspicion. I can remember that letters received by my mother in the 1950s and '60s were heavily censored and redacted. Some parcels were stopped, stolen or returned. I regret that my mother didn't keep some of them to show how much was redacted.

I was surprised to see the number of Vietnamese in the country, brought in to supplement the labour force.

I asked my uncle, through my father, about his experiences in Siberia and how he survived. He mentioned that the Russians needed workers in Siberia. If they asked for a carpenter, you volunteered. If they asked for a painter, you volunteered.

If you said you had a profession (like an accountant or a school teacher, which they didn't need) and you felt the work was below you, your food rations were cut. This food was given to those that worked.

He said that if you count the number of railway sleepers in the Trans-Siberian Railway you'll be close to the number of people who had died building it. Those who appeared a bit recalcitrant were taken to a tree and tied to it. In winter, they would slowly freeze to death. In summer, the midges were in plague proportions and would climb into their eyes, nose and ears. The person's hands would be tied. People would die screaming. The screams would echo through the forests.

The ground was permafrost and hard to dig by hand, and there were no earthmoving machines available. There were plenty of wolves and wild bears in Siberia. The bears sometimes came out of hibernation. There was no possibility of escape.

There were a few other things my uncle mentioned which I won't discuss here.

Everyone helped each other in Siberia. When they were released from Siberia and went home, they were surprised at the attitude of people they once knew, even some they once considered friends. The people released were shunned.

The Soviets had convinced the people not deported that those released were "enemies of the people" in order to justify why they deported them. It wasn't safe to be associated or seen with those who had been deported.

When I was first there, in the streets and shops there were queues everywhere, even in places where people had to pay their rent or buy vodka.

Abacuses were widely used in shops almost everywhere. I had thought it was only a child's toy when I was young.

I was surprised at my reaction when I saw some of the local young women. They were rugged up with coats that concealed all their feminine attributes. They wore hats and scarves. Some wore skirts under their coats. I asked Iveta when they would start to wear slacks. She replied: "When it gets below minus six."

All I could see was their eyes. What impacted me was how "sexy" a girl could look when all you're allowed to see are their eyes. Women in bikinis, which is normal in Australia, are a poor comparison.

When I wanted to change my son's plane ticket for an earlier flight, I waited patiently in the queue. A man pushed in when I was almost at the counter. I said to him the equivalent of "bugger off" and pointed my thumb over my shoulder to the end of the queue.

He said: "Sprechen ze Deutsch?" I was angry, it was cold, and I'd been standing politely in the queue for some time, so I replied loudly: "Noine". He asked where I was from. I replied, in perfect Latvian, that I was Australian – no one pushes me around.

Iveta told my Mum later about the incident and said how good my Latvian was when I was angry. She also was also surprised I reacted so aggressively.

On my flight home I met the same man again. We had to change airports and catch a bus. He helped me with my bags and paid for my bus ticket.

The market in Riga was in the old Zeppelin hangars built in the 1920s. It was, and still is, the largest market in Europe. There was hardly anything on the shelves. When a load of fish (carp) was dumped from a skip onto a shelf, a mass of people appeared as apparently there was nowhere else to buy it. The load disappeared within the hour.

There were street vendors with their small carts. They looked and dressed like they came from the Russian provinces – from I imagined the "…stan" countries.

There appeared to be many men wandering around who were obviously drunk. One complained to Iveta, in a drunken slur, about the terrible effect inflation was having on the price of vodka.

Iveta and Ojars had recently bought a second-hand car. It wasn't something I would even consider buying. To purchase a car in Russia, you were placed in a queue and waited. The car was Russian-made and looked a bit like an old Fiat. The brakes were faulty, and Ojars disconnected the hydraulic brake line to one of the wheels and bent it over on itself to stop it leaking.

Iveta drove the car faster than I would be game to on the ice-covered roads. She showed me many places where there used to be forts where, over Latvia's history, people were lined up and killed.

Iveta's family lived in a two-storey detached home that was still a work in progress as materials became available. Iveta said this was preferable to the high-rise apartments built by the Soviets.

I can't remember seeing a refrigerator, but Ojars proudly showed me his cellar under the house. Iveta's mother also tendered a small greenhouse in which she grew a few vegetables and flowers. I believe the flowerers were for the market, for some extra income.

They organised a "get together" dinner. I showed them how to make spaghetti bolognaise, which they had apparently never experienced before.

Food was available but it was scarce, and there was little variety. There were no luxury items like those from the delicatessens in Australia. I can't remember seeing any meat in the store. They made do with what there was.

They had pickled wild mushrooms which I found very tasty, and I may have eaten more than my share. I got the recipe and have made some myself in Australia. I don't use wild mushrooms, of course.

Butter wasn't available in the store, so Iveta took me to a dairy farm to buy milk. The farm was a bit dilapidated as it had been confiscated by the Russians and converted into a Kolkhoz. It was now presumably owned by everyone, but no one maintained it.

Iveta's mother took out a small wooden barrel with a capacity of about five litres. It had a shaft through the ends suspended in a frame and a crank handle at one end. She poured in the milk and churned it to make butter.

I remember my Mum and and her sister making butter and cheese in our old home in Bowral. They also had Russian-made alcohol called "Shampane" and "Conjak". They drank and sung the songs the Russians wouldn't allow them to sing in the "old days".

I was very tired due to the flying and the tours, and went to sleep on the couch.

The next day, Iveta took me to a Latvian graveyard. There were thousands of people buried there among the trees. The Latvians had, by tradition, been buried in a sacred forest.

My eyes immediately snapped on one "Olga Vidins". I was shocked she had the same first name as my mother. The lady buried there was my father's first wife. I later heard from Iveta that my father had paid for her gravestone.

Just before I left, we went to a store. Iveta pointed to a Latvian flag and asked if I wanted one. I reached for my wallet and she held my arm, insisting she pay for it.

When I was leaving, I stood at the corner of the house, in the snow under a Latvian flag, and Ojars took a photo.

When my father died, my mother buried him in Bowral Cemetery, in the town where we first arrived after we left the camp in Bathurst in February 1950. She had his plot dug deeper than normal. She told me that when she dies she wants to be buried on top of my father so that they can be as close as possible forever.

The Chinese believe that "no man can go through eternity without a woman". There is a long and complicated and interesting reasoning behind this.

Revisiting Latvia, 2024

In June 2024, I revisited Latvia for "Jani", the Summer Solstice. I didn't want to fly near or over the conflict zone of Russia or Ukraine. I flew with Finnair over the Arctic.

I was in Helsinki and had to walk to catch my connecting flight to Riga. It was a long way and I didn't have much time. When I got to customs there was a long queue in front of me. Those queuing were Chinese, Japanese or Korean holiday-makers. They had trouble with the customs officer, who was very patient, and took a long time to get through customs mainly due to language difficulties. I looked at my watch. The queue was long and there was a chicane to control the long line of people in front of me.

I asked the people on the other side of the chicane if I could "jump the queue". They were very polite, and I did this many times until I almost got to the counter.

I checked my watch again and hoped I had adjusted it correctly to allow for the time difference. I got to the counter just a few minutes before scheduled boarding for the connecting flight. The officer was very chatty and asked why I was travelling, if I had enjoyed the flight over, and where I was going to next, and when – "When did you arrive in Australia?" and "Do you have a family in Latvia?" She was very pleasant and seemed genuinely interested, but I was getting more anxious. It was boarding time for my connection. I may have been a bit abrupt and pointed to my watch.

I almost ran to the next gate. I had landed at the international terminal and the next flight was classed as domestic. It was a very long way away. I got there just after take-off. There were only a few people in the waiting lounge. I went to the counter to ask what I should do. The lady said the flight had been delayed an hour. It was a small propeller plane and I had a Business Class ticket. I sat down in the front row, and just before take-off they drew a curtain behind me. They offered me a glass of wine and a small snack for free.

Ineta

I planned to stay at my cousin Ineta's flat in a suburb of Riga. I rang to tell her I would be late.

She met me at the airport, and I recognised her with her small posy of flowers.

Her apartment was a bit old. It was built during the Russian occupation, I imagine in the 1950s. It was basic and not very luxurious. It had been her grandmother's before she had passed away.

It was a few storeys above ground level and had a basic kitchen with a stove and a fridge, and a very basic bathroom, a bedroom and a lounge.

We went to the city often, and I told Ineta that I wanted to eat something special. I was expecting she'd take me somewhere that served typical Latvian food. Instead, she suggested kebabs, pizza, "Subway" and hamburgers. I was very disappointed in her advice.

I told her that I didn't fly all the way to Latvia to eat what in Australia was considered "American fast food". I wanted something Mum would have cooked on very special occasions.

We eventually found some restaurants, but I don't think Ineta was impressed. She apparently preferred American-style food, which may have been novel there.

We visited the city a few times and saw the touristy things like the KGB buildings, where many people were detained and questioned. They played recorded tapes of people who were once internees. There were quite a few horror stories of what happened there.

To me, Riga was a beautiful city. It was established in 1201 and later became an important part of the Hanseatic League trade in the Baltic Sea.

The Daugava River, flowing past Riga and Jelgava, combined with the Dnieper Rivers, was one of the routes to the Black Sea and Constantinople used by both the Eastern and Swedish Vikings. It was very prosperous before World War I, and the city still has one of the largest numbers of Art Nouveau buildings in Europe. These buildings weren't damaged during the wars like the buildings in Jelgava, which were practically obliterated.

I visited the classic car museum. It had a replica Auto Union (which later became Audi), the famous 1930s race car. It had once had an original Auto Union but it was swapped for a replica when Audi wanted an original for their museum in Germany.

The museum also had many Russian-built cars of various vintages, and a Rolls Royce that had been given as a gift by the British to Leonid Brezhnev and had been damaged in a plot to kill him.

I arranged to get a copy of my mother's birth certificate, which was a requirement for me to obtain Latvian citizenship.

I wanted to visit Dviete, where my mother was born, and Kuldiga, which is mentioned frequently when referring to the stories of the Curonian influence in the region. I thought it may have had some association with my father's heritage.

But I didn't want to drive myself, and other events overtook us.

I was amazed at the transformation of Riga since my last visit. The city was now clean and there were many shops that were full of goods not seen on my first visit.

We went to the old Zeppelin hangar market. There were many stalls outside. It was well lit and I could see several coffee shops. The shelves were full of all sorts of goods and huge quantities of meat and fish not seen on my first visit.

There were no queues like on my earlier visit, except for a few people lining up for coffee and cake.

I had to slow down a bit as blisters were beginning to form on my feet due to the cobblestone streets.

I had on my old, well-worn-in RM Williams elastic-sided boots, which I believe I've had for over 20 years. They had never given me blisters.

The narrow cobblestone streets may have looked picturesque but they were a bit difficult for me to walk on. Public transport in Riga is very good – the best I've seen anywhere – and inexpensive. You could go anywhere you wanted to go on a tram or bus, and get on and off anywhere within a purchased time limit. I imagine I could have used it more effectively if I had known the city better and could read Latvian.

The taxi service (Bolt) was also excellent. You just install the app on your phone. It tracks your location, so it knows where you are. You type in where you want to go and the app gives you an approximate time the taxi will arrive and the approximate cost. It also gives you the taxi's number plate.

It was very different from the first time in Riga, when I had to remain concealed while Iveta negotiated a fare in American dollars.

I got lost, but only a few times.

Iveta

Iveta was my half-brother's daughter. She had guided me around on my first visit to Latvia.

Iveta picked me up from Ineta's apartment in Riga. She lived in Jelgava, where my father and his father had lived before the war. Her choice of car had been upgraded since my first visit. Both she and her husband were now driving a Lexus each. He was an architect and had designed and built their two-storey home.

Hill fort

Iveta took me to places of interest near Jelgava. One was the town of Dobele. I believe it was the place of the last stand of one of the Semigallian (Latvian tribes) against the Crusaders.

The Crusaders had laid siege to the hill fort. They didn't succeed, even after several attempts. They raided and then burnt down the village beside the fort. The townspeople fled to the fort. There was insufficient food and water to sustain them for the long siege.

The head noble or chief in the area, Nemesis, knew the Crusaders were after him and that if he left Latvia the siege would be lifted. He fled to Lithuania. He didn't know how long he would be away, and he knew his son may have grown up by the time he returned, so he gave his son his silver ring so he would recognise him when he returned.

The Teutonic Knights found out about this ring and began searching for the boy. The remaining Latvians then gave their sons a similar ring, to disguise the real son.

Since then, when a boy of Latvian descent comes of age he is given a "Nemesis" ring. I wear mine with pride. I also have a gold version. My son has one which he wears constantly – so does one of my daughter's sons. My youngest brother's sons also wear them, and my cousin has one as a wedding ring, with gold braid as the minor "rope".

I think I may have seen one of the original Nemesis rings. In the late 1990s, I went to an exhibition in Sydney of the treasures of the

Tsar. At the entrance to the exhibition was a glass case containing what looked like an ancient Nemesis ring.

I was surprised at the size of the fort. The Crusaders must have been terrified of the Semigallian tribes returning and attacking them.

Being a construction engineer, I immediately questioned how it was possibly built. Transport and sourcing of materials to site is a major consideration. My first question was where all the stones had come from. They had rounded shapes, which suggests they were sourced from a creek or river, not quarried. There was only a small creek and moat at the bottom of the fort. I can't image the stones came from there.

The other thing that intrigued me was where the lime to bind the stones had come from. Limestone has to be sourced and burnt to make lime. It can also be sourced from seashells, but we were a long way from the sea. Latvia is heavily forested, very flat and swampy, so how does one cart stones and limestone from far away?

The last questions was, where did the labour come from? It possibly came from the village of Dobele, but even then the village wasn't large. And how would the labourers be fed?

Most early structures in Latvia were made from the abundant trees. Working with stone was very different. If the labour to build the fort was sourced locally, they would have needed to up-skill. One couldn't take all the farmers as they were required to tend the fields to feed the townspeople and castle-builders.

In the surrounding area, there were several abandoned, raised mounds where hill forts had once stood. What intrigued me was how even the massive earth mounds were made. All that was left on the earth mounds was a plaque stating there was once a hill fort there.

Jelgava

From the hill fort, Iveta and I travelled to the home my father was born in. My father, Arvids, was born in Pienava Manor House in 1914 in the Dzukstes Parish of Latvia. I told Iveta I would like to see it.

It was a bit of a disappointment as it was down a long driveway shielded by large trees. From what I could see, it looked a bit dilapidated, but judging by the dogs barking, people still lived there.

Across the road from the house was a large Russian cemetery. I imagined the trees were planted in front of the house to conceal the cemetery across the road.

The battle in the Curonian pocket where this house was located was where the Germans and Russians had the last stand. The battle in the Curonian pocket in World War II still continued after peace was signed off.

I was disappointed at what little I could see of the house, but glad I had visited.

I visited the city of Jelgava, which had been almost completely destroyed during World War II. One street where my father lived as a boy had a curve following the river. It had been demolished by the Russians after the war and substituted with a straight road.

The city's Cathedral had only one of its walls still standing. Where the rest of the building had been flattened were inlaid bricks in a courtyard outlining where the other walls used to be.

There were several cleared but vacant blocks of land in the city. I imagine they were once owned by someone who had been deported, died or left the country. I regret that I didn't ask. My mind was overwhelmed with what my father told had me and what I imagined it would be like. It was the spectacle and fear of opening wounds.

Iveta arranged a Latvian-style BBQ with kebabs and invited several of my relatives. We had trouble communicating, but the daughter of my nephew Rolands, named Evelyn, could speak a little bit of English. She was still a young teenage schoolgirl, and her English was understandable but very slow and painful. Evelyn was keen to practice her English with a fluent English speaker. I imagine she already spoke Russian and Latvian well.

One of my father's sisters, Brigita, came from Riga by train to be there. She came to the airport to see me off the first time I was in Latvia. She wanted to talk but there were many other people there, and as she didn't speak English we didn't get a chance to talk

This time, she had bought me a bottle of Riga Melais (Black) Balsam. This spirit alcoholic beverage is a quintessential Latvian drink, as important to Latvia as Scotch Whisky is to Scotland. It was allegedly first developed in 1752 for medicinal purposes.

Again, with her broken English, we tried to converse. She wanted to say something and had many questions, but I really regret we didn't spend time together. From what I could understand, I believe she had been a set designer for the theatre and opera, and that she once travelled to New Zealand to set up a stage for a performance.

All my relatives were at least bilingual in Latvian and Russian. I told Evelyn that she was welcome to come to Australia for a holiday to refine and perfect her English. She was about the same age as the daughter of one of my younger brother's sons.

We went to a restaurant when travelling. It was mid-summer, so we ate "al fresco". To me, it was still cold, but the restaurant supplied a blanket with each chair so you could throw it over your shoulders. It was common to see blankets on the back of chairs outside in summer.

Both Iveta and her husband worked during the week, so I only stayed with them for the weekend.

Rita, Germany, 2024

My cousin Rita got a bit upset that I wasn't visiting her in Germany. I particularly wanted to be in Latvia to experience Latvia's most important festival, the Summer Solstice. Rita insisted I visit, and paid for my return flight from Riga to Germany.

I told her I'd reimburse her, her but she wouldn't have it. She and her husband, Ralph, picked me up at the airport and drove me to their home. I was a bit nervous at the speeds they were travelling on the Autobahn. Ralph got upset when someone wasn't driving at least 160 km per hour. He expressed his displeasure verbally. I noticed people were whizzing past us, even in small cars like the VW Golf.

I had picked up an international drivers' licence before leaving Australia, but any thought of driving in Germany at those speeds, in a strange car, on the "wrong side" of the road, with German road signs and in unfamiliar areas, was instantly dismissed.

Rita took me to the DP camp where I was born. It wasn't in Oldenburg as my passport stated but in a suburb just outside of it.

She arranged for me to get my birth certificate. After seeing it, I felt a bit nervous as my first name was spelt phonetically, as "Vidwoods", not "Vidvuds" as was on all my documents, including my Australian passport. I would need it to be spelt correctly to obtain Latvian citizenship. The lady issuing the documents was very helpful and pleasant, so I bought her a box of special chocolates.

When I submitted the birth certificate to the Latvian Department of Citizenship they rejected it as it was written in a foreign language (German) and that was unacceptable. I had it translated and notarised into the Latvian language and they spelt my name correctly.

I had heard a great deal about the bombing of Cologne during World War II and wanted to see the Cologne Cathedral. It was black outside from soot, I imagine from the old train station nearby.

I was amazed at the number of cathedrals and churches in Cologne, which from memory numbered about 160.

Another thing I noticed when we were driving in the region was that I could always see at least two, and sometimes three, church spires. I imagine that in the "old days" they were located so that people could go to church either by walking or by horse and buggy.

Rita took me to town a few times to meet with her old friends. We would eat, and drink various types of beer. I paid with my credit card, and Rita would pay a little extra cash as a tip.

Rita lived in a small town called Eiks, in the district of Merchernich. It was a mixture of a very old town and some new homes. It included a church (of course), where Ralph's mother was buried, and a large manor house. The streets were narrow and designed for horse and buggy.

We also visited Satzvey Castle, an ancient medieval castle. It had a huge door, and in the yard was a large black powder cannon aimed at the entrance gate. Some of the rooms were decorated as they supposedly were originally. There were flags or banners on the walls and dripping candles fitted on spoke wheels suspended with chains from the ceiling. The castle was now used for cultural events. It didn't appear to have any electric light fittings.

Another venue we visited was an ancient walled town in the region of Eifel, which is in a low mountain range.

Rita also took me to the place where she grew up and showed me the games the children played. In the town that was especially built for DPs was the church. I was told that the parson had been very helpful and compassionate to DPs.

Rita said it now seemed ridiculous but as a child there were many men in her neighbourhood who had an arm or leg missing. It had seemed normal to her. In her child's eyes, "complete men weren't real men".

We also visited Bonn, which had been the West German capital before the "wall fell" and Berlin became the capital again. Rita lived and worked in Bonn for a while.

We also visited the Latvian parson's wife, Gita Putice, who looked after the DPs in the estate. She was 88 years old and "sharp as a pin". She spoke many languages, including perfect English without any European accent. Her English was so good one would think she was an native speaker. To me, she seemed a very gentle and caring person.

She and her husband looked after the needs of traumatised, frightened, desperate people who had a sense of hopelessness, lonely and possibly with suicidal thoughts. Rita said that the parson and his wife devoted their all to their task.

I've been asked what Germany means to me. It never occurred to me to think this through. I was born there but left when I was about two years old. I visited twice, but only briefly – once for work and once for a holiday.

I once mentioned to a German that I was born there. He responded that I was only an "ersatz" German. I've been too involved in other things to think much about it. My work always dominated.

What surprised me was the effect on me of the visit to Germany. I worked for some time in Brisbane, Sydney, Canberra, Melbourne, Adelaide and Perth, then spent some time in Bangkok, Beijing and Shanghai. They're all interesting, beautiful cities. My short stay in Europe had a profound and unexpected effect on me. It was so surprising, as if something was being retrieved from my lost memory, probably buried in my genetics or DNA.

I quote William Wordsworth from his poem 'The Solitary Reaper':

> I wish my tongue could utter the thoughts that
> arise in me.

In Leipzig, I stayed in a palace that had been converted into a hotel. It was built before Captain Cook landed in Australia. Napoleon had stayed there during the Battle of the Nations.

I visited the Keller, where Goethe allegedly rode down the stairs on a barrel. I rubbed the pig's nose outside the door of the Keller. Doing this means you will return one day.

I walked the old city and visited the largest war memorial in Europe, just outside of town, dedicated to the defeat of Napoleon in the Battle of the Nations. This was the largest battle recorded in European History before World War I.

There is a church built there to commemorate the 25,000 Russians that died there. It's hardly mentioned in English history books, as is Waterloo, which was a smaller battle. The Duke of Wellington is accredited as the hero of Waterloo, when it was the Prussian Field Marshal Gebhard von Blucher who saved him.

I visited a castle in Saxony, where there were knights in full armour and swords re-enacting battle scenes. There was a lady clad in leather and a short skirt riding a horse bareback with a bow and arrows, hitting a target while the horse galloped.

There were several bands playing medieval songs using primitive musical instruments, including bagpipes. I bought a few CDs. I liked them, but when I later played them to Rita she said she didn't like them, and told me that Germans frown on people being loud and demonstrative.

One weekend, I caught a train from Leipzig to Weimar. It was an exceptionally beautiful medieval-style city. There were food stalls, traditional music, and beer on almost every street.

We also visited the medieval town of Eifel.

Riga has the largest collection of Art Nouveau buildings in the world.

Iveta and I were on a bus, and a lady older than me asked if I was American. I asked her why she thought so. She pointed to my Nemesis ring and said that only people from overseas with Latvian heritage wear them all the time.

There are also many palatial buildings outside of the town. It had now recovered from the Soviet era which I originally saw in 1991.

Apart from not being conversant with the languages, I never felt out of place. I feel really Australian but with European ancestry. I wonder if 'cosmopolitan' is the best description of me?

I flew back to Riga and caught the bus. For my last few days in Riga, I moved to a hotel closer to the main city. I'm an early riser and wanted to see and experience as much of the city as possible before I left.

I got lost only once. Returning to my hotel, I was standing in front of it when I asked a passing girl for directions. I had left the hotel on one side of the street and returned on the other, from the opposite direction … to me, the hotel looked different.

The girl gave me directions, and said: "Look behind you." I don't know what she thought, but she laughed.

I found a good restaurant on the riverbank. The food was excellent. I particularly enjoyed the beef tartare, which was made at the table, and washed it down with two glasses of French Champagne. I went to the same restaurant the next night and, seeing as I'd enjoyed it so much, had the same again.

Reflection on my life and lessons learnt

My father told me when I was very young: "One who hasn't made any mistakes also hasn't made anything."

Some people say that experience is a name for your mistakes. If this is correct, I've acquired a lot of experience.

The Chinese say words to the effect of: "Mistakes, if you learn from them, teach you wisdom."

My best engineering projects were all large ones where I had reasonable autonomy and worked with real professionals or people who knew their task, or the ones eager to learn.

All of the above went very well. I've managed two projects that have won excellence awards. Several others should have also been on the list but weren't submitted. Most people who worked on such projects said, when it was over, that they enjoyed working with me.

The owners of the smaller projects usually tried to micromanage me and put their personality on the project. They generally had less experience or expertise than I did. They may have been excellent in their own particular field of expertise, but some would regard them as the "B team" when it came to project development.

There's an old Australian saying that I believe summarises them: "You don't get a dog then bark yourself." Some of these small projects didn't go as well as I would have liked.

I try not to micromanage. As an engineering project or construction manager, I know I don't have expertise in everything. I choose, and delegate to, people who have more knowledge than I do in areas where I don't have time or expertise. On small projects, I didn't have the expert staff I normally had on "big projects".

One of the most important things I learnt was how to manage challenges and adversity. Overall, I think I managed the majority of the really big, important issues in life reasonably well.

I've thought a great deal about why many people I met who called themselves "an Australian" behaved the way the did (and sometimes still do).

My experience wasn't unique. Even now, I still hear an undertone of racism, sometimes covert but often overt, from people I meet.

Things that come to my mind in my case are:

- In the past, just before World War II, Australia was very isolated from the rest of the world, both physically and by the lack of global communication. Australians could be described as "living at the end of the world".
- Letters "home" to England "took forever" as they were delivered by sea freight. Literacy competency also limited this form of communication.
- Regular telephone services between Australia and Britain/ Europe began in 1924. Those early calls were very limited and expensive.
- Important news events from Australia and overseas were only displayed in cinemas or in old newspapers.
- Movies were almost always in English with an English theme, and the bad guys had a "foreign" accent and name.
- At the time, Aboriginal Australians were excluded from the National Census and were widely regarded by authorities as "primitive".

- Very few Australians were multilingual and didn't feel the need to learn another language.
- Overseas travel was once expensive and time-consuming. A voyage by ship took about six weeks one-way. The first four passengers came to Australia by plane in 1935, and it took them 12-and-a-half days. In 1947, after World War II, this improved. Planes could carry 29 passengers, with a flight time of 58 hours over more than four days. It still required seven stops.
- Attitudes are passed down through many generations.
- Sectarianism was rife. "Mixed marriages" were heavily frowned upon and strongly discouraged. Catholics and non-Catholics were even buried in different parts of the same cemetery.
- Even within Australia there was "the tyranny of distance". Australia is a big country, and it's a long way between capital cities. Travel between them was by boat or horse. The train rail gauges (track widths) when developed were different gauges between states. A continuous standard-gauge rail link between Melbourne and Sydney was only completed in 1962.
- There were no wars between the Australian states or with other countries, which would normally facilitate the large movement of people and ideas.
- Australia only became federated in 1901. There was practically no regular trade with other countries to facilitate the movement of ideas.
- Horse travel was common in Australia until the 1920s, and in rural areas it continued to be widely used into the 1940s. It was slow and limited in range.
- Until the 1920s, there were few cars and little service and infrastructure for cars to travel very far out of town. Only

- the very rich or people who needed cars for work could afford them, and automobiles were often unreliable.
- Pedal-powered radios for communication in the outback were developed in the late 1920s and became widely used in the 1930s.
- Before World War I, radio was in its infancy. In 1927, Amalgamated Wireless Australasia (AWA) conducted a series of transmissions to England. In the 1930s, the ABC had "synthetic cricket" that transmitted only the most important statistics of the game "by wire". The rest was recreated in the ABC studio.
- Approximately 62,000 Australians were killed in World War I and about 160,000 wounded, from a population of less than five million.
- About 30% of Australians lost their jobs during the Great Depression in the 1930s.
- There was fascism in Australia with the "New Guard", which was manifested by Francis De Groot cutting the ribbon on the opening of the Sydney Harbour Bridge in 1932. This was to embarrass Jack Lang of the Labor Party.
- Television wasn't introduced in Australia until 1956 when the Melbourne Olympics was screened. Even after that date, it was rare to have a TV until the mid-1960s.
- SBS began radio broadcasting in 1978, and SBS Television started in 1980.
- Arthur Calwell, Australia's first Immigration Minister, stated that all of us DPs would become Australians in five years' time, and that our children would all be Australians.

Many Australians, for the above reasons, had a myopic view of the rest of the world. Many considered Australia the best country in the world, so there was no need to change or adapt. I can understand people saying that if they haven't experienced anything else.

There is also still a bit of the "cultural cringe" in Australia.

Someone once said to me: "You don't have to scratch deep to find a bit of racism in Australia."

Apart from engineering, I have a very strong interest in history. People say words to the effect that those who disregard history are forced to relive it. You can currently find this manifested in the popularity of the leader of one particular political party.

The management of a country requires more skill than finishing school at 15, working as a barmaid then managing a fish and chips shop in a country town in Queensland. Her main support comes from Queensland and country New South Wales. She wants all newcomers to be like what she imagines she and her supporters to be. She claims new arrivals don't want to assimilate.

I believe she is very much like the people she criticises with her own version of fundamentalist, uncompromising views. I believe she believes she is absolutely right and those that disagree with her are absolutely wrong.

This attitude of some groups has resulted in conflicts that have lasted thousands of years. Regrettably, her party has significant support, and its main aim is to define us as what she imagines we once idyllically were to divide us.

An example of fostering division is the emphasis on any negative incident that is caused by someone with a non-Anglo-sounding name or who looks a bit "different".

Many Australians seem to be proud of their convict heritage, and lionise figures such as Ned Kelly, Ben Hall ("the Wild Colonial Boy") and Captain Starlight. We also need to recall the razor gangs of the 1920s.

It may be that I'm making excuses for some of this behaviour. I like to think that most of the initial reasons for it have now been circumvented, and change will be inevitable. I hope it will be for better.

Some people considered as "outsiders" gained a degree of acceptance due to their sporting prowess. Notable examples are Evonne Goolagong Cawley, Ash Barty, Cathy Freeman, the Konrads, Usman Khawaja, Lionel Rose, Sam Kerr and Kosta Tszyu.

I arrived in Australia before the Holden car was released. I was educated here, and have travelled and worked in more places in Australia than most people who call themselves "Aussies". But I'm still regarded here as not a "really true Aussie". The only time I'm identified as a "really true Aussie" is when I'm overseas.

When I was working in Bangkok, I was walking down a street on a Sunday. A Thai man came up to me and asked if I was Australian. I was surprised, and said yes. I asked how he guessed that. He pointed to my RM Williams boots.

In Beijing, many years later, I was staying at the Kempinski Hotel. I used to go down to get my boots polished. The shoe polisher said "Odalia", and pointed to my boots. "Odalia" means Australian in Mandarin.

Once, while I waiting in a queue for a taxi outside the hotel, an American woman called me, in a loud voice, "Crocodile Dundee".

In Papau New Guinea, Canadians, Americans, New Zealanders, Filipinos and nationals all identified us as a group of "Aussies".

While working in Adelaide, I stayed with an old man of Greek heritage. He was allegedly one of the richest men in South Australia. He made his money buying and selling real estate. One evening, I was sitting in his loungeroom. He was having a drink and eating canapés his wife had prepared, as we watched a replica of the HMS Endeavour sail past, up the Spencer Gulf.

We talked about many things. Then, during the conversation he said to me: "My parents came here after World War I fleeing the Turks. I was born on a farm in the bush in Australia in 1926. I came to Adelaide and now they still call me a bloody wog." After a few more drinks, he invited me to dinner. We drove to dinner in one of his Rolls Royces.

According to the 1921 Australian census, 51.8% of Australians were first- or second-generation migrants. One must ask what a "true Aussie" really is.

In the early 1980s, I was sent to manage a large construction project in Newcastle, New South Wales. I expected the city would be similar to Wollongong, i.e., steel and coal mining industry bases and being the second- and third-largest cities in New South Wales. Both have beautiful beaches, harbours and sea fronts.

I've had some people tell me that New South Wales really means "Newcastle, Sydney and Wollongong".

To my surprise, I was confronted by many people in Newcastle who said words to the effect of, "you're not from here" and "you're not one of us". It was the only time I was confronted like that in all the sites I worked at in Australia

Is someone who, for example, was born in Newcastle, whose parents and grandparents were born in Newcastle and who hasn't travelled much outside the immediate region except for the occasional holiday, really a "Novocastrian" or a "real true-blue Aussie"?

They're not someone who lives in the "bush", "off the sheep's back". They're not the "Crocodile Dundee" character. (Interestingly, this film was based on the character of Arvids Blumenthal, a man of Latvian decent.)

Tom Kruze (MBE), the mailman in outback Australia, featured in the 1954 film Back of Beyond.

They're not as typified by Steve Irwin or Paul Hogan.

They're not what someone thinks of as the typical "Aussie battler" as portrayed by Michael Caton in the film The Castle.

We look nostalgically at Dad and Dave in the 1920 film On Our Selection.

Are they someone whose ancestor arrived in Australia as an Afghan Cameleer almost 200 years ago, helping open up Australia?

We should also look at the 1928 Australian silent film The Birth of White Australia.

Are they one whose name is Louis Ah Mouy, a man who became very rich in the Victorian gold fields? He was one of the cofounders of the Commercial Bank of Australia, which merged with the Bank of New South Wales in 1982 to become Westpac.

We lionise the ANZACs, and the 416,809 Australians who enlisted for service in the first World War, representing 38.7% of the male population aged 18–44. They fought to preserve the British Empire which Australia was a part of – not specifically to defend Australia.

Of those who enlisted, 61,514 died, 166,811 were wounded, 4,098 went missing or became POWs, 87,865 suffered sickness, and I don't know how many had varying degrees of psychological and incapacitating injuries afterwards.

What is not recognised by many people is that thousands of men of German ancestry volunteered to become ANZACs. Many had Anglicised their names. John Monash, who led the Australians in World War I, was of German/Jewish ancestry.

Are they one of the approximately 1,000 Indigenous Australian soldiers who had at least one European ancestor who fought in World War I? These people were relegated as "blacks again" after the war.

People descended from the Chinese Amoy Shepherds also fought as ANZACs. Billy Sing was awarded the Distinguished Conduct Medal (DCM) after World War I.

Are they one of the "Ten Pound Poms" or "whingeing poms" and their descendants who arrived after World War II? (25% of whom went back "home" and had to repay the subsidy given to them to get them here).

Up to the 1960s, Australian citizens were still required to declare their nationality as "British", and continued to be British subjects up until 1984.

There are people such as those of Chinese descent who came to Australia during the Gold Rush in the 1850s, or the Sikhs from Punjab in the late 1800s who had grandparents born here, some of whom have intermarried. They're considered by some as not "real Australians".

A song we identify as quintessentially Australian, *Waltzing Matilda*, is about a man named Samuel Hoffmeister. He was a swagman who allegedly drowned himself in a billabong. His ghost is heard, but not his name, every time the song is sung.

I worked with many men, after I started work at the blast furnaces, who had lived through the Great Depression. One was a tall, skinny man who had eyes sunken in their sockets and wore boots without socks or laces. He wore a Jacky Howe shirt and a suit. His suit had torn pockets, and he held up his trousers, which didn't reach his boots, with a rope around his waist. He looked positively scary.

There was another man who would dig a shovel in the hot sand after a "cast" in the blast furnace a few times to clean it. He would then bang the shovel on the ground to remove any sand and would cook his steak, onion, tomato and eggs with lard in the shovel over the hot sand. "Steak wasn't cooked properly if it wasn't cooked on a shovel."

We had starlings in a crane that the driver said was spreading lice. He bought his shotgun to work to kill them on night shift.

I worked with another man who kept his bread and a half-opened tin of mouldy Irish stew in his tool locker, along with his gumboots, a sweaty furnace coat and asbestos rope. He would cook his lunch in a jaffle iron. "Bread is no good for a jaffle iron unless it's really stale."

Is an "Aussie" someone who just wraps themselves in an Australian flag and calls themself a true "Aussie"?

I've tried to understand why this was so nearly all my life. To me, contrary to mythical beliefs, there's no such person as a "typical Aussie". Most are all individuals. Figures show that 66.9% of people in Australia live in capital cities near the coast and the majority live in eastern Australia.

There is a distinct, individual uniqueness in all the places I've worked in Australia. I couldn't find a universal or national homogeneity. People in Kalgoorlie or Broken Hill are very different to those in Mt Isa (all mining towns), who are again different to those who live in the North Shore or Eastern suburbs of Sydney. They all speak a slightly different version of English, using different words, and their phraseology can be different.

People who live in Darwin, the capital city of the Northern Territory, are very different to those who live in Adelaide. The "City of Churches" began very differently to other Australian capital cities. There were no land grants, and people had to buy their land. No convict labour was used to establish the colony, unlike in the other states.

Darwin had a 6:1 ratio of Chinese to British White Australians when it was being established. Which ones are really "true Aussies?"

Some say "Aussies" are proud of their convict heritage. The question I ask is a simple mathematical one. Approximately 162,000 convicts were brought to Australia, and of these approximately 25,000 were women. What did the approximately 137,000 men do? If they paired up with all the available women, there still would be a deficit of approximately 117,000 women.

The few squatter's daughters would be strongly discouraged from marrying ex-convicts. The people that arrived with the gold rushes didn't bring many women with them. Did most of the ex-convicts die simply out without procreating?

In 2024, the annual immigration rate was 306,000, almost double the total of convicts who arrived in Australia from England.

Starting in 1848, approximately 3,000 Chinese were brought from Amoy (Xiamen) to work as shepherds in the expanding wool industry in Queensland, New South Wales and Victoria. There was a labour shortage, and freed convicts didn't want to work in the industry.

People from outside Australia who do monumental works in Australia have a history of being persecuted. To look at two notable cases:

- Canberra was designed by American architect Walter Burley Griffin. After designing Canberra, he ended up designing incinerators in Australia, before leaving.
- The iconic Opera House was designed by Danish Architect Jørn Utzon, who was "hounded" out of the country and never returned.

Was it a position Australians are renowned for – of cutting down what we perceive to be "tall poppies"?

Now that travel is relatively inexpensive, communication is easier. I believe and hope that, as a nation, we will see what other cultures can give us, and change, mature and grow.

Since the 1950s, we in Australia have changed a great deal. Some people, however, I believe will never change. They portray a certain arrogance. I believe the non-acceptance of fellow human beings who are superficially a bit different may be a sign of insecurity.

One thing I found very refreshing was when I had a group of New Zealanders ("Kiwis") working with me in Papua New Guinea. One of them was of Māori descent. The leading hand said to me: "He may be a bit sunburnt, but he's still one of us."

On one small project many years later, closer to home, I was in charge of upgrading a cement plant in Berrima, New South Wales.

I had a crew of people working away from home, from Newcastle and Maitland. To them, living in Moss Vale in the Southern Highlands was a unfamiliar, alien environment away from where they grew up.

They preferred to live in shared housing, except for two individuals. One was a gay man, who no one wanted to live with for fear of also being seen as gay. Otherwise, in all other respects he was accepted as one of "us". Another one wanted his girlfriend and two children to live with him. There were problems there also, as she felt isolated and had no friends in the area.

I don't believe they had much exposure to the regions outside of the Newcastle area. They worked long hours together, seven days a week, and ate, drank and took drugs together. They invariably got into fights with the "locals" who considered they were "poaching".

I also had a crew of local Kiwis who erected scaffolding. The Novocastrians looked down on the Kiwis. From what I'd heard from my crew, the two groups were fought continuously.

The project had a few hiccups, but generally went reasonably well. At the end of the project, I wanted to do something special for the whole crew. I asked the Kiwi Foreman if the Kiwis could put on a Mau Mau for everyone at my farm, which wasn't far away. He agreed, with the proviso that I supplied the pig and chickens.

On the day of the Mau, the cooks got lost on the way to the farm and, to my horror, didn't have a mobile phone. I got concerned, as it takes almost a day's cooking time, so I dug the pit with my tractor.

They eventually arrived about an hour later and redid everything I had done. They lit the fire, and when it burnt they created a hole in the middle. They jumped into the hot fire pit and scraped aside the ashes with just a wet towel over their heads, working almost frantically.

They inserted the contents into a basket and covered it with banana leaves, then ash and soil. They watched it. I offered them a beer, and they told me they were chosen because they didn't drink.

That evening, the rest of the Kiwis arrived, many of whom I hadn't seen before onsite. They came down the driveway singing, and the cooks responded by singing.

They cut the food and served it. We gathered inside to eat and noticed that the Māori stayed outside. I went outside and asked why. Their response was: "You are our guests, so you eat first." I was surprised, and told them that where I come from, it's customary that we all eat together, and to come in.

We started eating, and then one Kiwi stood up and said: "My brother would like to say something." We all went quiet, and felt humbled when he said something in Māori, then ended the speech with the word "Amen". Then they started eating. We felt like we were uncivilised barbarians.

We finished dinner, and there were no fights between the Māori and the Novocastrians even though there was a great deal of beer consumed. At the end, the senior person from the Māori group stood up and asked if he could do something special, and asked for quiet.

Two Māori then performed the "Haka". All the "white guys" were quiet and totally stunned. It's something I think the Novocastrians and I will never forget. It was such a powerful statement, and I felt really humbled.

After everyone went home, a mate of mine and I were reflecting, over a beer, on what we had experienced. Then a stranger arrived. I now assume he was a senior representing the Kiwis. He asked if everyone had behaved. We said it went well, and thanked him for an incredible experience.

For months and years after that event, the stone walls and solid timber roof of the farm seemed to echo the performance.

The attitude ideally for people should be: "I'm OK and you're OK".

For younger people, we have changed from a tea culture to a coffee culture, as a result of the Italian influence.

One can find greater varieties of food and cooking methods from other countries. "Meat and three veg" or meat pies and roasts on Sundays are no longer the standard fare. In Australian cities, one can find food from almost any country.

When I was younger, Chinese restaurants, now supplemented by Thai, Malaysian, Korean and Mongolian eateries, were more popular than fish and chips or McDonald's. The Asian versions in Australian restaurants are modified versions of the genuine, mainly to suit the Australian preference and palate.

In the 1890s, 30% of the cooks in Australia were of Chinese heritage.

When I was in Townsville with my Indian colleague some years ago, I wanted to go to an Indian restaurant with a native Indian. My colleague was from Chennai in the south of India. The food there, I was told, was very spicy.

The restaurant was run by a man who wore a turban. I assumed he was a Sikh from Northern India or Pakistan. He had Chennai Chicken on the menu. This I found unusual as Sikh's are usually vegetarians.

I asked my colleague, was it the real thing? He tasted a portion and said it wasn't. He went to the chef and challenged him. The chef said it was "Townsville Chennai Chicken".

Cooking shows on television, showing sometimes exotic cuisine or cooking methods, are very popular. We have, to me, regrettably, also developed a taste for fast food from the Americans. According to some reports, this is now decreasing, and many outlets are closing down.

In Australia, I've experienced eating crocodile, buffalo, camel, rabbit, emu, carp, goat, venison and donkey. It's all in the way it's cooked. Chinese and Mongolians can cook a tough steak like chuck steak that's as tender as fillet steak.

When I was first working in China in 2000, I was told that the Chinese don't kill or eat anything unless it's past its use-by date, i.e., the cow no longer produces milk or the chicken no longer lays eggs. When cooked, it's all very tender.

I'm surprised that we as a group don't eat more of our grass-fed, free-range "feral" animals that haven't been fed growth-promoting hormones.

In Europe and China, where carp originated, they're considered a delicacy if properly cooked. We seem to have some prejudice against carp because of the myths, they taste muddy, and they're the "rabbits of the rivers". Carp, however, are a plentiful free-range resource and, because they're damaging the environment, can be used as food instead of left on the riverbank or turned into fertiliser.

Carp was first brought to Europe from China because it was prolific and a good source of protein. I've been told that in Norway, carp is considered "top shelf" and much sought after.

We farm trout, salmon and tuna, and feed them artificially.

An elderly lady once told me that "if it wasn't for rabbits, in the depression we would have starved."

Sport has also changed in Australia. Originally, soccer was only played by men from ethnic clubs, i.e., Marconi, Olympic, Morley Windmills, etc. It has become Australia's highest participant sport, with approximately one million participants.

Women's and girls' participation in soccer in 2024 in Australia was 221,436. The game is played at scale by women, alongside sports such as football and cricket, which were once seen as exclusively male.

We show the World Cup and English football on television.

Women are biologically different to men. They now participate in the highest levels of government, in corporations, and in medicine and science. Historically, they were barred from these areas.

Half of all doctors registered in 2024 in Australia had foreign qualifications. My previous doctor was Vietnamese. She left her position after having two children. My current doctor is also female and comes from Iran. My cardiologist is from southern India, my kidney specialist is from Pakistan, and my urologist is from the Balkans.

Some people say they don't like the change, and prefer to go back to how Australia once was, whatever that means. They seem to have a nostalgic and filtered memory of an idealised past.

Some people say that when you come to Australia, you should leave all your baggage behind and forget what happened in your country of origin. Many of these people are still clinging to what they believe are their old British origins.

The Australian flag doesn't show our current diversity. It still has the British Union Jack in the top left-hand corner.

My suggestion for the flag is a similar concept, but with something in the top corner to indicate the unity of the national mix in Australia. It could also include something obviously Australian that is immediately recognisable, like a kangaroo. The Southern Cross could also be included.

The national anthem has been modified since conception. I believe the song by Athol Guy of "The Seekers" *I am Australian* may be more appropriate today. However, it should include a few extra verses to make it represent the current population.

The Australian republic referendum held in 1999 failed because most voters didn't want to become a republic. They voted to remain under the British monarchy.

I remember the swaggies, the old people who lived through the Great Depression that I'd met and worked with, and the bodgies, widgies, rockers, mods, go-go girls, etc. Where are they all now? I was there, with eyes wide open, and I definitely don't want to go back there.

I believe most people will change and adapt if they're accepted and see a need or advantage to do so. The "world is getting smaller", and we'll have to adapt to survive as a species.

It's also been my experience that if some people aren't accepted and are marginalised, some may find others in similar circumstances and group for mutual protection.

I remember one old "Aussie" (who was "dumped" here as an orphan at 15 years of age from Scotland) saying in the 1950s: "We may fight amongst ourselves now, but if we're attacked we'll all unite and fight as true Aussies."

I also believe I'm what may be described as a "realist", and use history as my reference.

Italy became Roman in the 3rd Century AD. The Roman Empire disintegrated into Nation States and only reunited in 1870. Italians still differentiate themselves if they come from North or South or from Trieste.

Germany only united in 1870. The Bavarians still treat the Prussians with suspicion.

There is Northern Ireland and the Republic of Ireland.

There is also the Middle East, which hasn't resolved its position for thousands of years.

Greece was the world's first democracy, but disintegrated.

I also know that we're generally very bad at predicting the future.

I look at 2,000 years ago. Who could predict one could use urine to make the explosive gunpowder. Some don't believe it even now.

One thousand years ago, the fear was that the world was going to end at midnight in the year 1000.

Five hundred years ago, Nostradamus made predictions of terrible things happening in 2026.

Two hundred years ago, Tomas Malthus in his *An Essay on the Principle of Population* made certain predictions.

Some of Jules Verne's absolute fantasies came true, but not in the way he predicted.

One hundred and twenty-five years ago, some scientists said: "We have invented everything that it is possible to invent."

Then there was the renowned thinker and writer Aldous Huxley and his book *Brave New World.*

George Orwell wrote *Animal Farm* and *Nineteen Eighty-Four.*

There is also the "Doomsday Clock," which was invented in 1947 and predicts how many minutes and seconds until doomsday.

Paul Ehrlich's 1968 book *The Population Bomb* said that the world would run out of food and hundreds of millions of people would starve in the next few years.

Who predicted that East and West Germany would reunite?

I remember attending a lecture at the University of Wollongong in the late 1970s where an immaculately dressed, articulate expert stated that we'll run out of coal in 45 years. We should stop mining coal now as we'll run out of coal which can be used to make chemicals and medicines.

Many predicted that in the year 2000, the world would come to an end, but if it didn't the "Millennium Bug" would destroy the world as we knew it. All the computers in the world would crash, and banks would no longer be able to work. The electricity grid, and everything that it powers, would collapse.

At the time, I was building a new coal mine in the Hunter Valley, and the client's representative, an electrical engineer, was terrified of the Millennium Bug. We spent a fortune to assure him it won't happen. It didn't.

I also like to consider myself as bit of an idealist. In Australia, I believe the next mature step would be to take the best of each of the new cultures and assimilate them into our own. Some people have an attitude of "us and them". The question is, who do we define as "us"?

The Snowy River Scheme required about 100,000 men with skills not then available in Australia. The surprising thing was that immigrants from different European countries worked with each other, in spite of being mortal enemies a few years before.

We have more in common than we have differences. Why do some people only seem to look for and concentrate on the small differences?

Some people have such strong ideas that they shut down anyone who differs from them. We've all tried to be inclusive, and had to change our language.

At university, I was accused of not being politically correct, and have been reprimanded for referring to people who were here before the "invasion" as "Aboriginal", which is derived from the Latin ab origine, which means "from the beginning". As Shakespeare wrote: "A rose by any other name is still a rose."

I think it's impossible to say or do something that doesn't offend at least someone. We need to be able to listen to others and not label those we disagree with as having some form of phobia. We seem to be breeding a "lot of koala bears", i.e., a large number of "protected species".

I was told a long time ago that "what doesn't break me makes me stronger". I'm a product of my genetics and my lived experiences and environment.

I've interacted (worked) with many different nationalities in Europe, Asia, the United States, Canada, and Papua New Guinea where some don't understand English. I didn't need a translator to know if they were angry, happy, upset, etc. It's relatively easy to distinguish a manufactured smile from a genuine one.

Sometimes, when people tried to use words, they would "get in the way". Language can be distorted by accents – we can miss understandings due to cultural differences. Incompleteness of the message arises when we assume they have a similar understanding and life experience.

Several acts of kindness I received in life I will never forget. While working in engineering construction, I had a farm and ran beef cattle for over 30 years. We need diversity. We need doctors and nurses, people who drive garbage trucks, the engineers, the shop assistants, and the educators from early learning to university level. We need those who look after people at the end of life. We also need the farmers, lawyers, police officers and administrators.

They're not all the same type of person or personality type, i.e., whatever "us" means.

If it wasn't for people who dared and were allowed to be different, we wouldn't have developed as a species. We wouldn't have developed agriculture if someone hadn't had the idea of collecting the best seeds and planting them.

Someone could choose clay, shape it and fire it to make pots.

Someone wouldn't have developed how to smelt copper, make bronze then later iron.

It was someone's idea that a wild horse could be tamed and the wheel invented.

There are also some negative aspects to some aspects because of some people's differences. There's an old joke about two country boys who go to the city for the first time. One says to the other: "They're all weird here, except us, but sometimes I worry about you also."

Many people believe all one needs is a faith and it is the answer. My opinion is that this faith has been good for some, but in the past (and currently) has been exploitative or used to divide us. I personally have experience of several charlatans that have influenced the vulnerable in my family.

I accept the attitude to change will be slow, as it will be intergenerational. If one doesn't see areas that can be improved, they will not try to improve them.

I believe that following the United States' lead – also a land of immigrants, with its values and norms – is definitely not the way to go.

The Americans I've met have a firm belief that the United States is the best country in the world. The rest of the world has nothing to teach them or there isn't any need for them to change. Generally, they believe they're something very special, and are intoxicated with their power. They also believe the world is an American, communist or third world, and that any form of perceived socialism is evil.

When they travel, they generally group or "cocoon" and stay in tourist hotels or construction camps (temporary portable accommodation installed and later removed during the construction phase) with other Americans.

Collectively, in the third quarter of 2025, the wealthiest of America's 1% held about $55 trillion in assets, roughly equal to the entire wealth held by the bottom 90% of Americans combined. I like to believe we're more equitable and egalitarian than that. We, as a nation, have to find our own way.

There would be hundreds of thousands, if not millions, of different stories from people that originated in Australia and those that migrated here. They can teach us a lot from all this diversity, and we can "cherry pick" the best.

I believe we definitely can adapt and change. I've seen the dramatic, almost unbelievable change in China from when I first worked there in 2001 to the second time in 2011.

When I was young and we got a wall-mounted telephone, I was so impressed. There was a day-time and an off-peak cost. Calls overseas were rare and prohibitively expensive. Now, we can call or send messages over a mobile phone overseas almost instantly.

We can read the latest news over the phone.

The danger I see now is too much information from uninformed and unverified sources, each with their own agenda and information deliberately designed to manipulate us. This often comes from social media and American entertainment. Social media can have a very dark side, if not managed.

Most of us have adapted or embraced electronically to the new technology. Now we have to adapt to the human side of our attitudes to others we don't classify as "us".

If we don't change or adapt, we'll stagnate or, worse still, go backwards or be dominated by others, with adverse consequences.

I consider myself "really Australian", but my make-up is founded on the many diverse generations of ancestors that came before me, from other countries, and from exposure to many other diverse nationalities and ideas. This is true for all Australians, even though many may not acknowledge it.

I like to imagine that Australia's First Nations people can also see some of the benefits outsiders have brought in, such as electricity, running or stored water, education, trade, transport, roads and medical services. The services they currently lack are true for all people who wish to live remotely, outside the cities.

I believe that a "treaty" where one group is perceived as getting more than another without adapting and "working for it" will deeply divide us. I believe our best interests are found in bringing all of us closer together. This means we have to change.

We expect all those that come to Australia to eventually become one of "us" and adopt our shared values. We will always have individual personalities and will always have to accept our differences. I ask, does "us" mean with all our current faults and prejudices?

I like to believe we are maturing.

We, however, as a nation, still have a very long way to go.

An example of taking the best available ingredients and making something uniquely Australian is the Pavlova, though Kiwis will say it is from New Zealand. Good ideas are always worth adopting. The Pavlova has a Russian name, and is made with eggs, a variety of fruit and berries, and whipped cream – ingredients that normally don't come together. What is in the toppings is not set – as long as it's the best in season and delicious.

I like to think that, from what I've seen, experienced and accepted, I don't have a myopic view of the world.

In my home, I have an Aboriginal dot painting from the Western Desert, artifacts and jewellery from Papua New Guinea, paintings from China, and, in a box, a book written in Chinese and English on silk.

I have bronzes from Thailand and China, Latvian jewellery of silver and amber, and wooden candelabra, boxes, clocks and more.

I have various flags from places I've worked. I have photographs, albeit not as good as I would have liked.

I had several what some people would consider almost sacred trees on the farm I used to own – Lebanese Cedar for an old friend, Oak, the Latvian male tree, Linden the female and Willow Chinese female and popular a Chinese male tree.

My wife is of Italian heritage. I've experienced and listened to many different cultures and tried to understand their values and why they have evolved. Everyone I've met has had some impact on me – some slight, others significant

My make-up is a "smorgasbord" of everyone I've ever known, with a few secret ingredients. It can take a long time, knowledge and skill, with many different ingredients, to make a good smorgasbord. It's not just like a meat pie and tomato sauce, where it can be easier to buy one ready-made.

My thanks go to those who came before me, to my beloved wife, Wanda, to my children, their partners, grandchildren and great-granddaughter, those who I consider past and present friends, and my colleagues, of whom there are too many to mention.

After what I've seen and experienced, with an open mind to the faults we currently have, I still believe Australia is the best country in the world. I also believe it has the potential to be even better.

In Australia, one can love a country and still criticise the areas that need improvement, to make it even better. In engineering terms, we call this process "quality assurance".

Appendix – Rita's letter

The letter below is from my cousin Rita. It was written while she was living in Germany, and regards her father, an uncle of mine. I've included the whole email, without alteration.

Dear Vid,

I actually meant to write a long time ago—at the latest after your two emails in September. I was very touched by how you described your situation after arriving in Australia. How difficult the living conditions were... in every respect. And despite all the difficulties, which could just as easily have depressed and discouraged people, I always experienced your family as warm and full of life.

It's either in the Dombrovskis genes, or an unwavering faith in God, or your family of origin was ultimately able to make the best of everything.

These thoughts have been going through my head again now that you've asked me about my father. I myself hardly have any concrete memories of him anymore. He died when I wasn't even eight years old. Even before that, he was often absent. He was either working shifts or was in some kind of rehabilitation program. At the time, I wasn't given a clear explanation as to why. In retrospect, I think it was often about addiction treatment.

Once he had to go to a hospital for pneumonia or pleurisy, and that was probably right after I was born.

When I think about it, it was more normal than unusual for my father to be away at health resorts. I remember postcards he wrote in Latvian would arrive regularly. My mother would read them aloud, and then I would correct her pronunciation. It's a shame I couldn't retain my language skills from back then. But after I started school, there were no close persons left with whom I could speak Latvian.

Speaking of school: I started in the summer of 1968. My father died in February 1969. Where was he when I started school?

I basically only know about the loss of his leg from my mother's stories. Of course, I saw it and remember the visits to the medical supply store, where we often had to go for adjustments/ modifications to his prosthesis, but I only learned how it happened later. According to Mom, it was a classic war injury, caused by a—probably— Russian soldier. Mom always said that Dad had always emphasised that he wasn't angry with the Russian. After all, he was just doing his job.

Anyway, this injury apparently led to my father

being sent to a military hospital in southern Germany. And I once heard this story from your mother: In this hospital, someone pricked up his ears at the name Dombrovskis and told Dad that he had met some people with the same name in a camp in northern Germany. Through further conversation, Dad was certain that they must be his parents and siblings.

As Olga told me, it was probably around Easter, and for reasons I've forgotten, there was a curfew. But my father was now driven by the desire and the intention to see his family again, whose fate he had known nothing about until then.

Somehow he managed to get out of the military hospital with his amputated, barely healed leg, to hitch a ride despite the curfew, and to make his way to Oldenburg. There, they probably saw each other for the last time. Our grandparents, your parents, Sascha, as well as Helena and Peter, had already applied to emigrate by then. My father was supposed to come along too. But as a war veteran, that was, of course, much more difficult to arrange. Olga also mentioned that Dad later received an emigration permit, but that these papers were stolen. I have no idea if that's true. Perhaps my father lost heart... who knows. Mom never told me anything more specific about it.

I only learned much later how my parents even met. Mom worked in a lawyer's household in Oldenburg-Etzhorn, a neighbouring district of Ohmstede, where the camp was located. At some point, she must have answered a personal ad in the newspaper. Dad was glad she didn't mind his missing leg, and Mom was impressed by his independence. She hadn't seen that from her brother or father. My father must have been a cheerful, sociable person. So she accepted that her new love smoked and drank.

Over time, the drinking obviously became a problem. Many encounters with other people had only this common denominator. Often they were "old comrades" who had shared the same fate and had thus been washed up in Oldenburg. At the other end of the street, a kiosk with a pub had opened after the apartment blocks were built. Dad could often be found there, too. On the whole, things usually went well as long as he "only" kept his blood alcohol level at the necessary level. However, there was one type of schnapps that he couldn't tolerate at all, and then he would become abusive and insulting to Mom. The next day, he would regularly be ashamed and apologise profusely. I only have a vague recollection of such a scene. This problem was usually kept from me.

Only years after Dad's death, and when I had a better understanding of the background, did Mom tell me how difficult it often was for her? Despite understanding that a young man who had lost his leg, his home, and his family as a soldier, she still suffered. To make matters worse, my father had irregular work, so there was no financial security, my mother had to earn extra money through piecework at home, and it was solely on her narrow shoulders to organise a somewhat stable life—especially for me.

His death was ultimately a result of his disability and a visit to a pub. However, it was always emphasised that he didn't drink a drop that evening at the end of January. The icy path was enough to throw him off balance; he could no longer stand with one real leg and a prosthesis on the other, and suffered a triple fracture in his healthy leg. He died in the hospital a few days later.

At the time, the explanation given to me was that his recovery would have been problematic and that Dad, faced with the prospect of possibly ending up in a wheelchair, had lost his will to live. Later, Mom admitted that his circulatory system couldn't withstand the withdrawal symptoms. She had pleaded with the hospital staff to give him either alcohol or substitute medication, but apparently, that wasn't standard practice back then.

Oops – this is what came of the few lines I wanted and needed to write you.

Now you're faced with the problem of deciding what you can and want to use.

But thank you for the task – having to summarise everything (well, the essentials of my memories) has, I think, also made some things about myself clearer.

All the best
Rita